Charismatic Leadership and Missional Change

American Society of Missiology Monograph Series

Series Editor, James R. Krabill

The ASM Monograph Series provides a forum for publishing quality dissertations and studies in the field of missiology. Collaborating with Pickwick Publications—a division of Wipf and Stock Publishers of Eugene, Oregon—the American Society of Missiology selects high quality dissertations and other monographic studies that offer research materials in mission studies for scholars, mission and church leaders, and the academic community at large. The ASM seeks scholarly work for publication in the series that throws light on issues confronting Christian world mission in its cultural, social, historical, biblical, and theological dimensions.

Missiology is an academic field that brings together scholars whose professional training ranges from doctoral-level preparation in areas such as Scripture, history and sociology of religions, anthropology, theology, international relations, interreligious interchange, mission history, inculturation, and church law. The American Society of Missiology, which sponsors this series, is an ecumenical body drawing members from Independent and Ecumenical Protestant, Catholic, Orthodox, and other traditions. Members of the ASM are united by their commitment to reflect on and do scholarly work relating to both mission history and the present-day mission of the church. The ASM Monograph Series aims to publish works of exceptional merit on specialized topics, with particular attention given to work by younger scholars, the dissemination and publication of which is difficult under the economic pressures of standard publishing models.

Persons seeking information about the ASM or the guidelines for having their dissertations considered for publication in the ASM Monograph Series should consult the Society's website—www.asmweb.org.

Members of the ASM Monograph Committee who approved this book are:

Robert Gallagher, Associate Professor of Intercultural Studies and Director of MA (Intercultural Studies), Wheaton College

Paul Kollman, Associate Professor of Theology and Executive Director Center for Social Concerns (CSC), University of Notre Dame

RECENTLY PUBLISHED IN THE ASM MONOGRAPH SERIES

Lila W. Balisky, *Songs of Ethiopia's Tesfaye Gabbiso: Singing with Understanding in Babylon, the Meantime, and Zion*

Kevin George Hovey, *Guiding Light: Contributions of Alan R. Tippett Toward the Development and Dissemination of Twentieth-Century Missiology*

Charismatic Leadership and Missional Change

Mission-Actional Ministry in a Multiethnic Church

CRAIG S. HENDRICKSON

FOREWORD BY
MICHAEL O. EMERSON

American Society of Missiology
Series vol. 43

☙PICKWICK *Publications* · Eugene, Oregon

CHARISMATIC LEADERSHIP AND MISSIONAL CHANGE
Mission-Actional Ministry in a Multiethnic Church

American Society of Missiology Series 43

Copyright © 2020 Craig S. Hendrickson. All rights reserved. Except for brief quotations in critical publications or reviews, no part of this book may be reproduced in any manner without prior written permission from the publisher. Write: Permissions, Wipf and Stock Publishers, 199 W. 8th Ave., Suite 3, Eugene, OR 97401.

Pickwick Publications
An Imprint of Wipf and Stock Publishers
199 W. 8th Ave., Suite 3
Eugene, OR 97401

www.wipfandstock.com

PAPERBACK ISBN: 978-1-5326-7819-6
HARDCOVER ISBN: 978-1-5326-7820-2
EBOOK ISBN: 978-1-5326-7821-9

Cataloguing-in-Publication data:

Names: Hendrickson, Craig S., author. | Emerson, Michael O., foreword.

Title: Charismatic Leadership and Missional Change : Mission-Actional Ministry in a Multiethnic Church / by Craig S. Hendrickson ; foreword by Michael O. Emerson.

Description: Eugene, OR: Pickwick Publications, 2020 | American Society of Missiology Series 43 | Includes bibliographical references.

Identifiers: ISBN 978-1-5326-7819-6 (paperback) | ISBN 978-1-5326-7820-2 (hardcover) | ISBN 978-1-5326-7821-9 (ebook)

Subjects: LCSH: Ethnicity—Religious aspects—Christianity. | Multiculturalism—Religious aspects—Christianity. | Christian leadership. | Mission of the church.

Classification: BV639.M56 H46 2020 (print) | BV639.M56 (ebook)

Manufactured in the U.S.A.   03/11/20

Dedication

This book is dedicated to Reverend Johnny Collins (deceased), a man of God whose dream of pastoring a multiethnic church took him from Los Angeles, California, through Reno, Nevada, all the way north to Edmonton, Alberta. Your passion and faithfulness in the ministry and to me helped me to receive my call into pastoral ministry and ultimately helped to birth my own vision for multiethnic ministry. You modeled faithfulness in a way that few do in today's world, and I am forever grateful for how you invested in me as a young man and new believer. Your legacy lives on through me and through this work, hopefully impacting many for years to come.

Contents

List of Tables and Figures | ix
Foreword by Michael O. Emerson | xi
Preface | xiii
Acknowledgments | xv

Introduction | 1
1. The Lighthouse in Its Urban Context | 14
2. The Lighthouse's Journey: Merging Attractional with Missional | 23
3. Leadership Resources Driving Change at The Lighthouse | 38
4. Adaptive Challenges at The Lighthouse | 64
5. Missiological Implications of the Leadership Praxis at The Lighthouse | 81
6. Making the Case for Interpretive Leadership at The Lighthouse | 114

Conclusion | 122

Appendix A: Interview Participants | 129
Appendix B: Leadership Interview Questionnaire | 131
Appendix C: Congregational Survey | 132
Bibliography | 137

Tables and Figures

Table 1: Pastor Steve's Positive Leadership Indicators | 39
Table 2: The Five Leadership Boxes | 41
Table 3: Ethnicity and Level of Church Involvement | 75

Figure 1: Respondents' Age | 17
Figure 2: Respondents' Ethnicity | 17
Figure 3: Respondents' Current Financial Status | 18
Figure 4: Respondents' Proximity to The Lighthouse | 19
Figure 5: Respondents' Time at Current Residence | 20
Figure 6: Respondents' Years of Attendance | 21
Figure 7: Respondents' Church Involvement | 22
Figure 8: The Main Priority of Our Church | 53
Figure 9: Our Church's Priority to Love and Serve Our Neighbors | 53
Figure 10: Our Church Should Form Partnerships | 54
Figure 11: Neighbor Involvement | 65
Figure 12: Changes in Neighbor Involvement | 66
Figure 13: Responsibility for Outreach | 68
Figure 14: Mission Focus of the Church | 69
Figure 15: Permeable Church Boundaries in Missional Identity Formation | 105

Tables and Figures

Figure 16: Forming Missional Identity in Construction Sites | 106

Figure 17: The Nature of Interpretive Work in Construction Sites | 108

Figure 18: Identifying Adaptive Challenges through Interpretive Work | 110

Figure 19: Participating in God's Initiatives as a Multiethnic Church | 111

Foreword

FOR NEARLY A QUARTER century, my colleagues and I have studied congregations—churches, synagogues, mosques, and more. We have particularly focused on understanding how Christian congregations come to be racially and ethnically diverse, why they are difficult to sustain, where they can go awry, and the incredible impacts they can have.

Always the answers come back to the same factor: leadership. There is simply no getting around the fact that dynamic, charismatic, vision-driven, people-focused leadership is the driver of people catching the vision for congregational racial diversity and justice, for understanding the biblical call, for being motivated to make changes and sustain growth, and for being mission-minded.

This is why I cannot sing enough the praises of *Charismatic Leadership and Missional Change*. Born out of deep theological reflection, decades of experience, and careful study, Dr. Craig Hendrickson guides us on a journey into effective leadership of multiethnic ministries. He has been forged in the fire, prepared to write this book. The lessons learned, if applied, will lead to dramatically healthier multiethnic congregations, relationships, and ministry.

The need is dire. We live in a time of racial, ethnic, political, and cultural divisions so severe that they threaten to shred our societies as we know them. We are ripping at the seams, and our technologies, medias, and talking heads all appear to only encourage ever more seam ripping. We need to find leaders—followers of Christ—who understand that they are called to be Seam Repairers of God. They must serve in the urban, suburban, and

Foreword

rural areas of this vast nation and world, understand where the seams are ripping, and get to work repairing.

To do so, as we know, Christian leaders must have increasing cultural competency. They must have on the full armor of God but take off their cultural clothing. They must be able to wear Joseph's coat of many cultural colors.

The present reality means we truly need *Charismatic Leadership and Missional Change*. Our two thousand-year-old church adapts its timeless message to an ever-changing age as people writhe about trying to find happiness, meaning, and purpose. They are constantly blown about chasing the latest craze, the newest technology, and the trendiest ways.

As Martin Luther King used to say, our technologies have allowed us our world to become a neighborhood, but not a brotherhood. Put in more modern speak, as our world has grown smaller, people of all backgrounds are more likely to live somewhere other than their homeland, and our cities have become the locals where the world meets. But we don't know yet know how to live together. We don't yet know how to care for one another. We don't yet know how to create a true tapestry of God's creation.

Read *Charismatic Leadership and Missional Change*, teach and apply its lessons, and help us get closer to the Beloved Community to which God has so long called us. That is our calling, and that is the great promise of this book.

Michael O. Emerson, PhD

Professor of Sociology, the University of Illinois at Chicago, and author of *Divided by Faith*, *United by Faith*, and *People of the Dream*.

Preface

THIS BOOK IS BORN out of personal experience. Over the past twenty-five years, I have served in various volunteer and vocational ministry roles, most of which have occurred in multiethnic or cross-cultural environments. During that time, I have served as a pastor and as a volunteer leader in both mono- and multiethnic churches, and also as a leadership coach and consultant in the areas of multiethnic and missional ministry with Church Resource Ministries. I have also spent the last nineteen years in an interracial marriage and family, where many of my intercultural competencies have been born and/or refined. Through these experiences, I have seen the challenges as well as the benefits and joy of serving in and belonging to a multiethnic community of faith and family. These experiences, combined with deep and ongoing theological reflection, have formed some deep convictions within my heart and mind about multiethnic ministry. I believe that multiethnic congregations offer incredible potential for carrying out highly effective mission in America's increasingly diverse urban centers. I also believe that they can be places of redemptive healing where a broken and fragmented society can witness what true racial and spiritual healing can look like. It is also my deep conviction, however, that the level to which these things occur is dependent on effective leadership. It is this leadership challenge that has inspired my research and that causes me to seek how to better equip leaders to carry out these tasks. My hope is that this contribution will do just that.

Acknowledgments

I WOULD LIKE TO thank my beloved wife Mary, my best friend and number one supporter. You've stood beside me through numerous transitions and pushed me when I didn't feel like writing. You picked up the slack in our family life when necessary so that I could write while you were working full-time. Without your sacrifice, there is no way I would have been able to do what was necessary to see this process through. I am thankful for you every day. I love you!

I would also like to thank my beautiful and spirited daughter Amaya. You sacrificed lots of daddy-daughter time while I was writing. You also cheered me on to the finish line and helped inspire me to keep writing when I was tired. Thank you honey! I love you very much and look forward to making up the time we missed.

I would also like to thank Pastors Steve and Ella, the pastoral and ministry staff, the lay leaders I interviewed, and the congregation at The Lighthouse. Your willingness to participate in the research that inspired this book and put yourselves under the microscope enabled me to carry out my research and ultimately to write this book. I can never thank you enough for your partnership in this endeavor.

Finally, I would like to thank my mentor, Dan Shaw, and my dissertation committee members, Mark Lau Branson and Jude Tiersma Watson. Your unwavering confidence in my ability to complete my research . . . your relentless exhortations to keep me on track . . . your insights that helped refine my writing skills . . . and your encouragement and support are a huge reason that this book is finally complete. I would not be here without you. Thank you to each of you!

Introduction

As I walked through the doors of the Edmonton Community Worship Hour (ECWH) in the fall of 1994, I immediately said to myself, "I'm home. This is what church is supposed to look like." While not a large church, the sanctuary was buzzing with energy in anticipation of the worship service that was about to begin. But more importantly to me, it was filled with an incredible diversity that I had yet to experience in a local church during my first eighteen months as a new Christian. I saw people of every hue talking and laughing together, hugging one another, praying together. It was a beautiful picture of what I believed the church was supposed to be—people "from every nation, tribe, people, and language, standing before the throne" (Rev 7:9), worshipping God. My experience at ECWH over the next two years would solidify my passion and vision for multiethnic ministry and launched me on my journey toward pastoring, consulting, and ultimately researching multiethnic congregations.

Several years later, as I sat across the desk from Pastor Steve, listening as he shared his story about leading his church of approximately one hundred mainly white congregants to become a thriving multiethnic church of more than 700 weekly worshippers, my vision for a specific research project was born. I began to wonder what it would look like for a pastor or team of pastors to lead a multiethnic church toward a more missional form of ministry in its community. I had been introduced to the "missional church"[1] discussion several years earlier while in seminary at Regent College in 1999, and had been on a journey of discovery ever since. After

1. Guder, *Missional Church*.

a difficult time in my first pastorate trying to help revitalize a declining historic church in Long Beach, California, I had become intrigued by the idea of moving churches beyond attractional approaches centering on the Sunday worship experience. Instead, I sought to move them toward a more missional model of ministry focused on joining God's activities outside of the church walls in their diverse neighborhoods. As I listened to Pastor Steve share how he had led The Lighthouse from an attractional approach into a multiplication model focused on church planting and, ultimately, toward an approach that he called missional, I realized that I may have found a unique situation to explore the relationship between my two passions in ministry—multiethnic and missional.[2]

As I began to investigate the viability of conducting research at The Lighthouse over the upcoming months, two factors made the decision rather straightforward. First, by commonly used standards of measurement, The Lighthouse is one of the most culturally, economically, and generationally diverse evangelical churches in North America. It has no single ethnic group consisting of more than 31 percent of weekly attendance in their main worship gatherings, and is on a journey toward deeper intercultural life and intentionally sharing power among the various ethnic groups present.[3] Second, it also has a reputation as one of the few thriving and missionally vibrant evangelical churches in Port City, where I was currently living with my family. When I considered this with the fact Pastor Steve had been leading a process of missional change for the past several years, and that I had complete access to the leadership, congregation, and documents of the church due to an ongoing relationship with Pastor Steve and the church, my choice was clear.

SETTING THE STAGE FOR RESEARCH AT THE LIGHTHOUSE

As I began to formulate my research agenda through a broad literature review, I was somewhat surprised to see that at that point in time, no one else had taken up this task. Instead, I found two growing fields of study that were developing separately and were catering to different groups of

---

2. Pastor Steve, The Lighthouse, and other names contained within this book are pseudonyms in as much as it is my desire to protect the reputation of all leaders involved in this case study.

3. See DeYoung et al., *United by Faith*; Emerson, *People of the Dream*; Ortiz, *One New People*.

Introduction

leaders. The multiethnic church phenomenon, for example, had seen a significant increase in scholarly inquiry over the previous two decades. This is due in large part to an increase in the number of multiethnic congregations in North American urban contexts that continue to be shaped by urbanization, globalization and migration, and increased intercultural interaction. It is also due to the fact that multiethnic congregations offer fertile research grounds to scholars interested in issues of racial reconciliation and social healing, approaches toward intercultural leadership, and congregational mission in culturally diverse urban environments. The result has been an increasingly varied list of scholarly works that continues to grow with each passing year. Several scholars, for example, have extensively explored the racial and cultural dynamics that influence congregational life in multiethnic churches through case studies and large scale mixed methods research.[4] Other practitioners and scholars have explored how to lead multiethnic congregations in the midst of these dynamics.[5] These writings have been helpful and have provided a valuable foundation upon which to build further research.

Over roughly the same period of time, the missional church discussion also gained significant momentum among those interested in seeing the church regain her missional vitality in a culture that is becoming increasingly post-Christian. Beginning with Darrell Guder's work in 1998,[6] there has been a plethora of books released discussing what it means for a church or leader to be missional. Alan Roxburgh and Fred Romanuk,[7] for example, provide a blueprint for how pastors can become missional leaders as they move their churches toward missional ministry. Likewise, Craig Van Gelder[8] shows pastors how to develop Spirit-led, contextually appropriate ministry in their communities. These and numerous other works have contributed significantly toward understanding how churches can discern and participate in God's missional initiatives in their communities.

---

4. See DeYoung et al., *United by Faith*; Christerson, Edwards, and Emerson, *Against All Odds*; Emerson, *People of the Dream*; Garces-Foley, *Crossing the Ethnic Divide*; Edwards, *Elusive Dream*.

5. See Law, *Wolf Shall Dwell*; Foster, *Embracing Diversity*; Branson and Martinez, *Churches, Cultures, and Leadership*; Smith, *Post-Black and Post-White Church*; Sanders, *Bridging the Diversity Gap*; Loritts, *Right Color*; Gray, *High Definition Leader*.

6. Guder, *Missional Church*.

7. Roxburgh and Romanuk, *Missional Leader*.

8. Van Gelder, *Ministry*.

Charismatic Leadership and Missional Change

What is particularly notable in the missional church writings is how the discussion has departed from the congregational leadership literature that has promoted top-down, leader-centered approaches to leadership dependent on the skills and wisdom of the pastor. Much of the congregational leadership literature has emphasized the need for a charismatic leader to initiate and drive the change process as congregations seek to engage their communities in mission. Conversely, the missional church discussion has emphasized the need for leaders to include the people of God in the change process to increase their adaptive capacity and more effectively mobilize their congregations into missional ministry. Mark Lau Branson,[9] for example, highlights the importance of the entire community of faith discerning the Spirit's works as they discover and form new meanings and practices together through praxis. This work of shaping a "community of interpreters" creates shared ownership between leaders and congregants and taps into the wisdom and discernment of the entire faith community instead of just one leader. Accordingly, a more complete picture of the context can be discerned and possible missional responses formulated collectively as the congregation functions as a true learning organization.

Despite the fact that the multiethnic and missional church discussions have developed largely alongside one another, at the time of my research, no empirical studies had explored the intersection between missional leadership and multiethnic congregational studies. While authors like Van Gelder, Roxburgh, and Romanuk suggested that contextually appropriate missional ministry calls local congregations to engage ethnically diverse contexts through multiethnic ministry, they did not flesh out the specifics of what this might look like. I was able to find two attempts to bridge these conversations theoretically, however. The first is an article I wrote exploring the relationship between missional leadership and multiethnic ministry through the lens of Ronald Heifetz and Marty Linsky's adaptive leadership framework.[10] Within this article, I suggest that particular adaptive challenges arise when those leading multiethnic congregations employ top-down, leader-centered forms of charismatic leadership. I then suggest that Branson's paradigm of interpretive leadership can potentially address these challenges and help multiethnic congregations attain higher levels of adaptive capacity and missionally vitality.[11]

9. Branson, *Ecclesiology and Leadership*.
10. Heifetz and Linsky, *Leadership on the Line*.
11. Hendrickson, "Using Charisma to Shape Interpretive Communities."

Introduction

The second attempt is a book by Mark Lau Branson and Juan Martinez. Utilizing Branson's leadership triad, they construct an approach to leadership that moves those in multiethnic churches toward deeper intercultural life and meaningful engagement with their neighbors. The goal of leadership, they suggest, is to shape "environments in which the everyday people of the church find that their own imaginations can be engaged by God's initiatives for them and their neighbors."[12] While the diverse sociocultural frameworks that shape the leadership environment in multiethnic churches create unique challenges for accomplishing this goal, their thorough treatment of these frameworks within a communal, praxis-based approach to leadership suggested a plausible pathway forward. Along with my own preliminary work, Branson and Martinez provide a theoretical bridge between these two distinct conversations—a bridge that ultimately helped inspire the unique nature of the research that I conducted at The Lighthouse.

STUDYING MISSIONAL CHANGE AT THE LIGHTHOUSE

As I began to formulate my research agenda in light of my reading and my experience at The Lighthouse, I began to realize that my research could have significance not just for my own studies but also for the church's leadership and a larger missiological discussion that I wished to contribute toward. I realized, for example, that my research could reveal specific insights into how church leadership at The Lighthouse could more effectively liberate and utilize the collective gifts and wisdom of their diverse membership as they continued to reshape their mission praxis in biblically faithful and contextually appropriate ways. I also believed that my findings might challenge current conceptions of congregational leadership that emphasize top-down forms of charismatic leadership as the preferred model for engaging local congregations into missional ministry. Finally, I believed that my research could provide a theoretical foundation upon which further research could be conducted to explore the value of interpretive leadership for facilitating missional innovation among congregants in multiethnic congregations.

With these goals in mind, I designed a case study[13] to explore how the pastoral leadership approach at The Lighthouse engaged ethnically diverse

---

12. Branson and Martinez, *Churches, Cultures, and Leadership*, 231.
13. Yin, *Case Study*.

congregants in the process of missional change in Port City, USA. To carry out this task, I explored four specific research questions that set parameters for my inquiry:

1. What is the nature of missional change occurring at The Lighthouse?
2. Why have pastors led missional change the way they have at The Lighthouse?
3. What is the nature of ethnic diversity present at The Lighthouse?
4. How has pastoral leadership fostered or impeded ethnically diverse congregants' involvement in the process?

To answer these questions, I collected data in two phases, utilizing two primary and two secondary methods. Phase one involved conducting interviews with pastoral staff and selected lay leadership and was supplemented by participant observation and source document analysis. Phase two consisted of a survey administered to the entire congregation.

During phase one of my data collection, I conducted fourteen semi-structured interviews—nine with the pastoral and ministry staff, and five with selected members of the leadership council and other lay leaders.[14] Each interview lasted between forty-five to ninety minutes and consisted of open-ended questions exploring the values, beliefs, and practices of each individual leader, as well as the leadership culture, missional focus, and practices of the church.[15] I began by interviewing the senior pastor, which gave me understanding into his leadership philosophy; provided me with a broad view of the church's leadership culture and mission praxis; and helped me identify four recent missional initiatives to explore further to understand the leadership process that led to their inception: (1) The Lighthouse Community Center; (2) a new community garden; (3) the Volunteer Service Corps (VSC); and (4) the Micro Enterprise Charter Academy (MECA). As I began to explore these initiatives through interviews with other pastors and ministry staff leaders who were involved, I gained valuable insights into: (1) the church's ongoing shift in its mission praxis; (2) the decision-making process surrounding new missional initiatives; and (3) the theological and cultural assumptions informing those decisions. I was also able to identify the specific lay leaders that I needed to interview to supplement my interviews with the pastoral and ministry staff.

14. See Appendix A.
15. See Appendix B.

Introduction

As the interviews progressed, I narrowed the focus of my questions to dig deeper into specific decision-making processes, theological assumptions, and participants' roles in specific missional initiatives during their time at the church. I supplemented these interviews with data generated from observations I made over four and a half years as a church member and one year as a part-time ministry staff member, as well as direct observations while sitting in on one Leadership Council meeting, four weekly staff meetings, and several Sunday services over a two-month period of time. I also analyzed several documents collected throughout this phase of research detailing the church's mission praxis and history, including budgets, the church's mission, vision, and values statements, emails and leadership lessons from the pastor to the staff, and various other documents that revealed insights into the specific missional initiatives that I examined.

After completing the first phase of data collection and my preliminary data analysis, I used analytical coding to identify themes to explore among the congregation. During the second phase of research, I then explored these themes utilizing a twenty-question, self-administered survey in the congregation during the three main Sunday services on a single Sunday.[16] I received 525 completed surveys from the 670 adults who were in attendance, which, when considered in light of multiple people attending all three services, yielded between a 78–90 percent response rate. I then sorted and entered the completed paper surveys manually into Survey Monkey and ran cross-tabulations on respondents' answers so that I could compare the results to my initial findings from phase one.

INTERPRETING MISSIONAL CHANGE AT THE LIGHTHOUSE

As I continued to reflect more deeply on the themes that emerged in the data, I applied an integrated theoretical framework to interpret the data centering on Heifetz and Linsky's approach toward adaptive leadership. At the heart of adaptive leadership is a leader's ability to distinguish adaptive challenges from technical problems. Technical problems are those that can be addressed with current knowledge and skills possessed by the experts in the organization. The problem is straightforward and can usually be resolved by a change in strategy by leadership. With an adaptive challenge, on the other hand, the nature of the problem resides within the people in the

---

16. See Appendix C.

organization, and it involves changing attitudes, values, and behaviors of those people. Because there is a new environment demanding an adaptive leap that threatens the existence of the organization if things do not change, technical solutions applied by the experts will not work. Instead, "the people with the problem" need to become "the people with the solution,"[17] as they internalize, own, and resolve the challenge by acquiring new skills and capacities and engage experiments beyond the technical solutions that have been tried in the past.[18]

According to Heifetz and Linsky, leaders can distinguish an adaptive challenge from a technical problem, or discern which aspects of a challenge are adaptive or technical, by "getting on the balcony" to gain perspective on what is actually going on in the situation. Utilizing this analogy, they suggest that a leader needs to remove him or herself from a situation like a dancer from a dance floor, even if only for a moment, so that he or she can gain perspective on the system and patterns in a situation.[19] This is important, for misdiagnosing an adaptive challenge as a technical problem can contribute toward interventions that do not address the real nature of the issue. But it is also important in another way. Gaining perspective also enables a leader to discern what type of adaptive challenge the leader/organization is facing.

Heifetz, Grashow, and Linsky suggest four adaptive archetypes that consistently plague organizations and leaders. The first is a "gap between espoused values and behaviors," which brings the people in an organization face-to-face with their real priorities as they identify how their behavior differs from what they say they value and believe.[20] Closing this gap can be painful, disrupting normal patterns of behavior for leaders and followers alike. Consequently, leaders and others in positions of influence often leave the gap unaddressed or try to apply technical solutions to assuage their dissonance in an attempt to avoid the drastic changes that might be necessary to solve the problem.

The second archetype is the presence of "competing commitments" that come into conflict with one another. These commitments usually prevent a true win-win situation and require leaders to "make painful

---

17. Heifetz and Linsky, *Leadership on the Line*, 127.
18. Heifetz and Linsky, *Leadership on the Line*, 13–14.
19. Heifetz and Linsky, *Leadership on the Line*, 54.
20. Heifetz, Grashow, and Linsky, *Adaptive Leadership*, 78.

choices that favor some constituencies while hurting others."[21] Because of the pain involved in the hard decisions necessary to resolve these types of situations, many leaders simply avoid making them or try to enact a compromise that ultimately satisfies no one. When this occurs, the organization's commitments remain in opposition with one another, preventing it from achieving congruence.

A third archetype identified by the authors is "speaking the unspeakable." What they mean by this is that there are usually two conversations going on when the members of an organization come together—one that is said publicly, and another that is going inside of individuals' heads. Much of this inner conversation is left unsaid because what is considered unspeakable could create tension or conflict that will need to be addressed. These unspoken priorities are essential, however, for moving an organization forward in the face of shifting priorities or contextual conditions.[22]

The fourth adaptive archetype they identify is "work avoidance." To avoid the discomfort that comes from initiating systemic change, people in an organization will often put the blame on some external force, create a committee or taskforce with no real power to effect change, change the subject when difficult topics arise, or continue to apply technical solutions to adaptive challenges. They engage in these strategies to avoid the truly difficult adaptive work necessary to address the challenge.[23]

Addressing any of these challenges effectively requires leaders to get off the balcony and re-engage the situation by creating a holding environment, which Heifetz and Linsky define as "a space formed by a network of relationships within which people can tackle tough, sometimes divisive questions without flying apart."[24] While holding environments can take many different forms depending on the context, the key is that they need to provide relative emotional and relational safety for participants to address the difficult challenges characteristic of adaptive work. Creating this space enables adaptive work to be carried out by those who need to engage it most—the people in the organization with whom the problem resides. This presents a conundrum of sorts, however, as leaders tend to be judged by their ability to provide solutions to the problems people are facing. Leaders must resist this urge, however, or they run the risk of providing a technical

---

21. Heifetz, Grashow, and Linsky, *Adaptive Leadership*, 81.
22. Heifetz, Grashow, and Linsky, *Adaptive Leadership*, 82.
23. Heifetz, Grashow, and Linsky, *Adaptive Leadership*, 84.
24. Heifetz and Linsky, *Leadership on the Line*, 102.

solution to an adaptive challenge, which provides temporary relief to the issue at best. The task of "giving the work back to the people," then, becomes a central leadership task, as "solutions are achieved when the people with the problem . . . become the people with the solution."[25]

As I explored how the pastoral leadership approach engaged ethnically diverse congregants in the process of missional change at The Lighthouse, then, I was particularly interested in: (1) identifying any adaptive challenges the congregation was facing due the pastoral leadership approach in the church; (2) determining how, or if, the pastoral staff identified and diagnosed the nature of those adaptive challenges; and (3) understanding any approaches taken to address those adaptive challenges. My analysis revealed three significant adaptive challenges at The Lighthouse, which I will discuss in detail in chapter 4. What I found, however, was that I needed to supplement Heifetz and Linsky's framework with two more theoretical approaches to more deeply understand the nature of the adaptive challenges and missional change occurring at The Lighthouse—Stephen Cornell and Douglas Hartmann's understanding of the nature of construction sites, and Claudia Straus and Naomi Quinn's understanding of cultural schema.

According to Cornell and Hartmann, a construction site is an environment, process, or institution where racial and ethnic identities form over time. They identify six such sites where this process of racial/ethnic identity formation occurs: (1) politics; (2) labor markets; (3) residential space; (4) social institutions; (5) culture; and (6) daily experience.[26] Within each of these sites, specific groups face various opportunities and constraints that interact with their own interests and capital as they "cope with the situations they encounter, pursue their objectives, make sense of the world around them, and identify themselves and others."[27] Accordingly, as a social institution, a local congregation is itself a construction site where identities are shaped at a group level.

In light of this understanding, I suggest that the process of missional change in a congregation can best be understood as a process of missional identity formation that takes place over time. In other words, as the people of God allow the Spirit to reshape their identity as a called, gathered, and sent people through praxis—an iterative, ongoing series of actions and reflection on those actions over time—they might begin to participate

25. Heifetz and Linsky, *Leadership on the Line*, 127.

26. Cornell and Hartmann, *Ethnicity and Race*, 169–209.

27. Cornell and Hartmann, *Ethnicity and Race*, 211–12.

Introduction

more intentionally and faithfully in God's redemptive initiatives in their local context and world. As Craig Van Gelder puts it, "The church is. The church does what it is. The church organizes what it does."[28] Accordingly, I suggest that leaders seeking to engage their congregations in a process of missional change need to set up construction sites so that a new missional identity can be formed among the people of God. This can only happen, however, in a safe environment where competing commitments and any perceived gaps between espoused values and actual behaviors relating to missional identity can be explored and challenged. In other words, construction sites need to be a place where discourse can occur, resulting in new meanings and practices.

The connection between my understanding of construction sites and Heifetz and Linsky's concept of a holding environment should by now be apparent. Both are spaces within the congregation (relational, physical, or processual) where difficult conversations relating to change can occur. Both are spaces within a congregation where people can explore who they are, what they believe, and what they value in order to identify who they need to become and how they need to respond more faithfully to God's initiatives among them. In other words, they both relate to forming and reforming identity among the people of God. In light of this similarity, the distinction I am making between these two concepts may seem moot. The distinction in language I am making is important, however, as it more clearly communicates how I understand the relationship between values, perceptions, assumptions, and beliefs with behaviors and practices in congregational life.

The final piece of my theoretical framework is Strauss and Quinn's approach toward cultural schema as understood through connectivity theory, which provides the heuristic theory to analyze and explain certain underlying causes of the adaptive challenges facing The Lighthouse. Cultural schemas are those learned mental structures shared by a group of people that organize related pieces of our knowledge to help us make sense of our world. They are developed through similarly mediated social experiences as people make their way through the world experientially and ultimately shape the way people define and pursue their self-interests. Culture, then, becomes "a name for all of the learned schemas that are shared by some people, as well as of the diverse things from which these schemas are learned."[29]

28. Van Gelder, *Ministry*, 17.
29. Strauss and Quinn, *Cultural Meaning*, 7.

Understood through connectivity theory, schemas are highly context sensitive because they are the result of a whole network of learned associations from past experiences that process information holistically. When a specific event or situation occurs, this network is activated in an attempt to provide an interpretation that will satisfy as many of the constraining factors as possible. Thus, connectionist networks are both regulated and improvisational because they are not only guided by previously learned patterns of associations but also created instantaneously on the spot.[30] Thus, meanings are produced by the schemas we have at the moment, and because situations can change, which activates different patterns of networks, meanings can be variable among both individuals and groups from context to context.[31]

Meanings are best understood, then, as momentary states produced through an interaction between schemas (intrapersonal mental structures) and structures (extra-personal). They are consequently psychological but are the result of this interaction and, in turn, the result of previous such interactions. In other words, "what something means to somebody depends on exactly what they are experiencing at the moment and the interpretive framework they bring to the moment as a result of their past experiences at the moment."[32] Meanings become cultural when they are widely shared and frequently recurring interpretations of events or objects that are "evoked in people as a result of their similar life experiences."

Cultural meaning, then, is highly context sensitive and variable. In a congregational context like The Lighthouse, then, it is important to understand the context and how the sociocultural forces within that context impinge upon the congregation. For example, how do prevailing cultural models of leadership contribute toward the leadership approach in the congregation? How do the diverse cultural assumptions about leadership held by ethnically diverse congregants interact with the actual practice of leadership in the congregation? In other words, what cultural schemas are informing leadership values and practices within the congregation, and how are those schemas shaping the particular adaptive challenges being faced by the congregation as it goes through the process of missional change? As we will see in chapter 4, these are salient questions not just for understanding

---

30. Strauss and Quinn, *Cultural Meaning*, 53–54.
31. Strauss and Quinn, *Cultural Meaning*, 83.
32. Strauss and Quinn, *Cultural Meaning*, 48.

the nature of adaptive challenges but also for understanding the process of missional change at The Lighthouse.

OVERVIEW OF THE BOOK

Throughout the rest of this book, I describe the rationale, process, and results of the case study research that I conducted at The Lighthouse. In chapter 1, I describe my research site, which includes the demographics of The Lighthouse and its immediate urban context in Port City, USA. In chapter 2, I provide an overview of The Lighthouse's journey from a primarily attractional model of ministry to its current praxis that I identify as mission-actional. In chapter 3, I then describe the way that Pastor Steve and the pastoral staff have led the church to its current praxis, paying special attention to the leadership resources they have used to shape the process.

In chapter 4, I then shift to a deeper level of analysis by identifying the adaptive challenges the church is facing as a result of the leadership style employed at the church. In chapter 5, I bring my findings into conversation with the missional church literature and scripture by discussing the contribution my work makes to the conversation surrounding missional leadership and multiethnic churches. In chapter 6, I then make a case for the value of interpretive leadership at the Lighthouse by presenting several conclusions from my findings. Finally, I briefly discuss the implications of my research for missional leadership at The Lighthouse and other multiethnic congregations, present my recommendations for further research, and give some closing thoughts in my conclusion.

1

The Lighthouse in Its Urban Context

NORTH PORT CITY: THE LIGHTHOUSE'S MISSION CONTEXT

As you walk around the streets of Port City, you cannot help but be struck by the diversity. While it is segregated along racial lines like most major metropolitan areas in the United States, it is not unusual to pass by people representing at least three or four different ethnic groups while taking a walk on an average street on any given day. Officially, it is comprised of roughly 42 percent Hispanics, 28.1 percent Caucasians, 12.5 percent African-Americans, 12.7 percent Asians, 0.9 percent Hawaiian and Pacific Islander, and 3.4 percent of people from other ethnic backgrounds.[1] By all accounts, then, it is one of the most diverse cities in the United States.

Though the immediate neighborhood surrounding the church reflects the overall ethnic diversity characteristic of Port City as a whole, it does so in different proportions. This is due to the fact that the zip code comprising the area of North Port City is a gateway community for immigrants that has seen rapid growth reaching back into the Nineties.[2] This rapid growth—due in part to large numbers of Hispanics, Asians, and Pacific Islanders flooding into the largely affordable area as older white residents move away or die—has resulted in higher than average numbers of these groups residing in the church's immediate area. The tract immediately surrounding

---

1. US Census Bureau, "American Community Survey."
2. Humphrey, "City of Long Beach," 9.

the church, for example, saw 8 percent growth among Asians and Pacific Islanders, 211 percent growth among Hispanics and other groups, and a 27 percent decline among Anglos during the Nineties. A study by the Department of Planning & Building in Port City predicts that these trends will continue into the foreseeable future, estimating that the area will become increasingly Hispanic, African American, and Asian and will likely see an influx of young, educated residents due to the relative affordability of housing in the area. The most current data supports this claim, with the area right now consisting of 57.5 percent Hispanics, 8.6 percent White, 19.2 percent Black, 10.9 percent Asian, and 1.4 percent Hawaiian/Pacific Islanders.[3]

The result of this continual growth and demographic shifting is that the church currently sits at the juncture of several distinct ethnic and class communities. My direct experience in the neighborhood confirms this and also leads me to believe that it has a higher than average underserved population, an above average crime rate, and several ethnically distinct gangs that compete for control of the surrounding turf. In fact, according to local residents, there are at least six separate gangs located within one square mile of the church. Humphrey agrees with this, noting that North Port City experiences many of the problems associated with overcrowding in densely populated urban areas.[4]

DEMOGRAPHICS AT THE LIGHTHOUSE

While the church has not successfully reached all of the distinct ethnic communities in its immediate context, it has never-the-less enjoyed a great deal of success reaching a number of different demographics in its community. The church is well known and respected in the Port City faith community as one of only a handful of growing evangelical churches in the city, and has a reputation in the city and within its denomination as a missionally vibrant church in a spiritually challenging city. Unlike many churches that grow primarily through transfer growth, for example, The Lighthouse appears to have a noteworthy rate of conversion growth. While exact statistics are not available, I personally observed several people respond to the salvation call at the end of services each week I was in attendance. Consequently, the church has grown from approximately one-hundred, mostly Anglo members when the current pastor took over in 1991, to approximately 700 diverse attendees in three Sunday services and over seventy-five children

3. US Census Bureau, "American Community Survey."
4. Humphrey, "City of Long Beach," 18.

in its Sunday school and nursery. These numbers would undoubtedly be higher were it not for space limitations and the church's commitment to church planting, which I will discuss further in chapter 2.

Diversity at The Lighthouse

When you walk through the doors for the first time at The Lighthouse, you immediately notice the diversity. The church has significant numbers of Hispanics, Caucasians, African Americans, Africans, Asians, and Pacific Islanders of all ages, and it is immediately apparent that there is no visible majority group in the congregation. It is also apparent that the congregation comprises a great deal of multinational diversity. During one service dubbed "International Sunday" in early 2009, for example, there were greetings given in over thirty languages by congregants as the microphone was passed around the sanctuary. Finally, according to church giving records and anecdotal evidence, the regular attendees include lower income through upper-middle class constituents with the majority of members consisting of the working and middle-classes. Overall, The Lighthouse appears to be one of the most diverse churches in the United States.[5]

The data generated through my survey in phase two of my research process confirms these observations. For example, survey respondents included significant numbers of congregants from a variety of ages; from Under-18 youth through 65+ seniors. The two largest groups, self-identified as 36–49 and 50–64, combined for 61 percent of the sample. The two smallest groups were on the fringes, with those identifying as 65+ at 6.5 percent, and those identifying as Under 18 at 9.2 percent.

---

5. See DeYoung et al., *United by Faith*, 74.

The Lighthouse in Its Urban Context

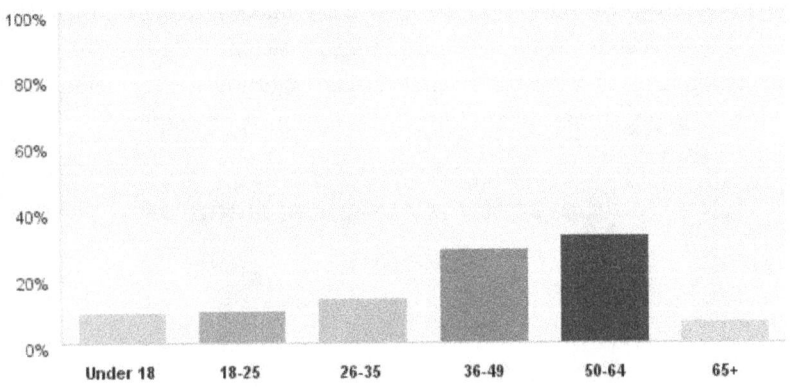

Ethnically, 30.4 percent of respondents self-identified as Caucasian, 27.5 percent as African American, 19.4 percent as Hispanic, 14 percent as Asian/Pacific Islander, and 13.9 percent from various other ethnic backgrounds including Africans, Native Americans, Caribbean Islanders, and those identifying as multiracial.

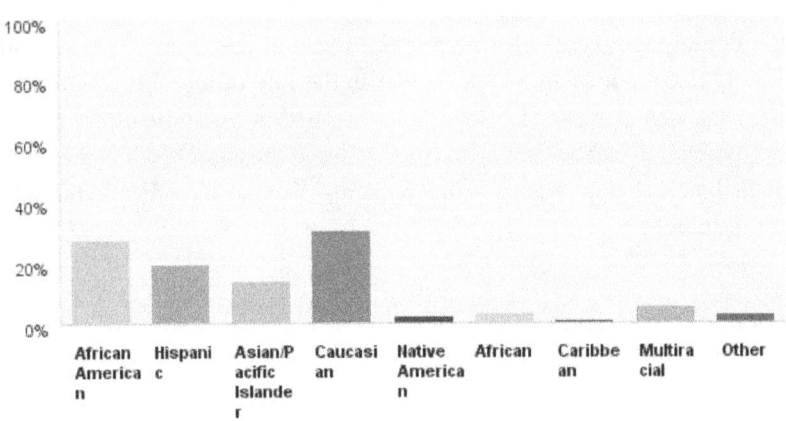

Finally, the data also revealed that while the majority of respondents feel that they are comfortable financially (52.9 percent), over one-quarter (26.7 percent) feel like they are barely making enough to sustain themselves, and almost one-in-five are either not making enough to pay their bills or are receiving some type of financial assistance. Participants in this survey, then, reveal a level of diversity at The Lighthouse that is seldom seen in local congregations in the North American mission context.[6]

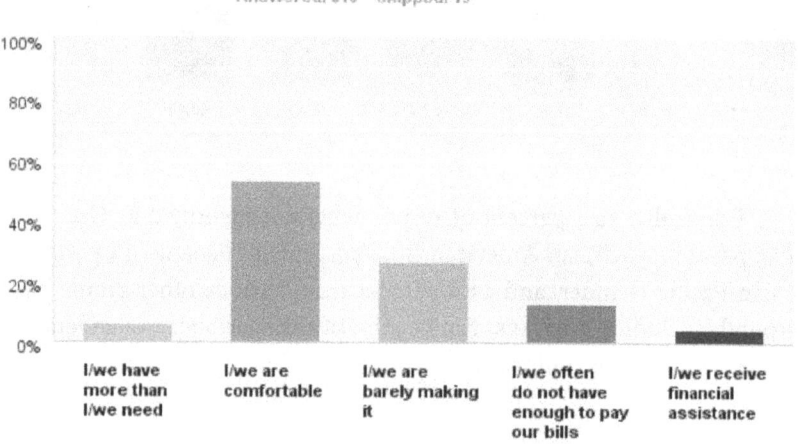

Proximity and Mobility of the Congregation

The demographic data also reveals the reach of the church into its community and surrounding area as well as the rate of mobility among congregants. 14.1 percent of respondents live within one-mile of the church, 29.8 percent live between one to three miles of the church, while the largest single block of respondents—39.6 percent—live between four to ten miles of the church.

---

6. DeYoung et al., *United by Faith*, 3.

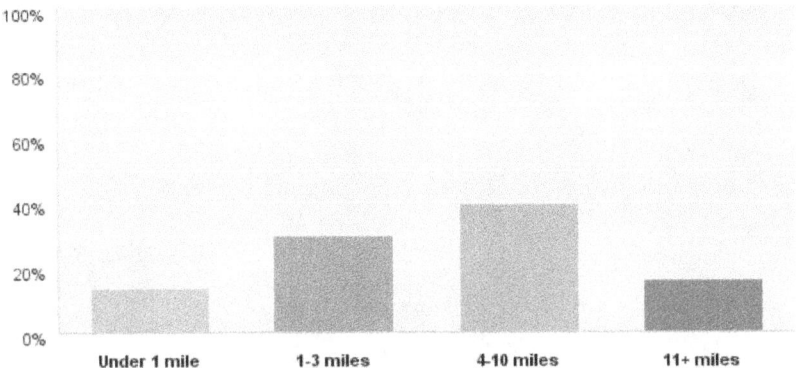

This supports findings that I will discuss in later chapters regarding the church's shift in mission focus to a more community-based ministry, driven by the emerging missional theology of place among church leadership.

Conversely, it also indicates that the church still draws heavily from the edges of and outside of the greater Port city area, demonstrating the regional appeal of a growing multiethnic church. This could either be due to the expanding reach of the church or the mobility of people that the church is currently reaching. For example, 37.6 percent of respondents indicated that they have lived in their current residence for less than three years.

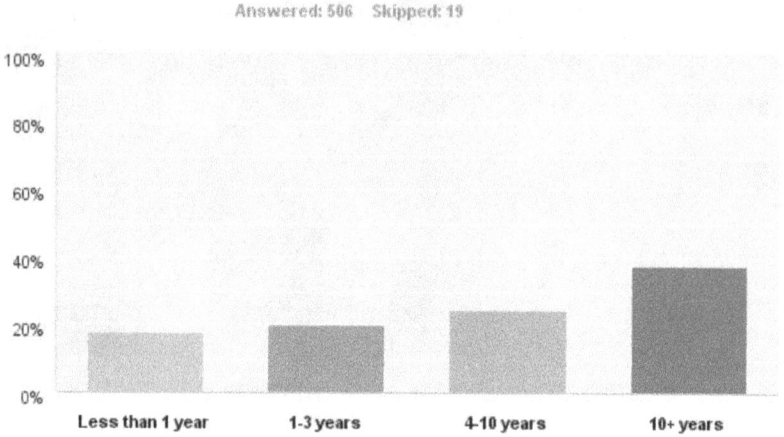

This figure could represent a number of factors, including migration of people looking for work or to better their standard of living, or white flight out of the church's surrounding neighborhood that has become increasingly Hispanic, African American, and Asian/Pacific Islander. The data is inconclusive on this issue, yet seems to indicate that elements of both may be involved.

Tenure and Involvement at The Lighthouse

Finally, the data reveals that the church maintains a balance of new and long-term members. 22 percent of respondents indicate that they have attended the church for less than one year, 24.2 percent between one to three years, and over 30.5 percent have attended between four to ten years. The remaining 23.3 percent have attended for eleven years or more.

The Lighthouse in Its Urban Context

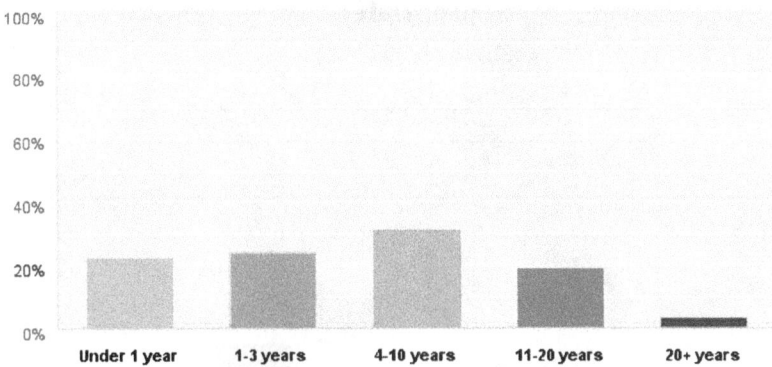

These figures are interesting when you combine them with respondents' level of involvement in the church. In spite of the fact that almost 80 percent of respondents have been in the church for over one year, and over half (53.6 percent) for four years or longer, only 35.2 percent indicate that they are members, less than one-in-five (18.7 percent) are serving on a ministry team, and just under one-in-six (16.3 percent) are connected to a small group. Thus, while attendance is high, like many other churches in North America, involvement beyond the Sunday worship service attendance is limited.

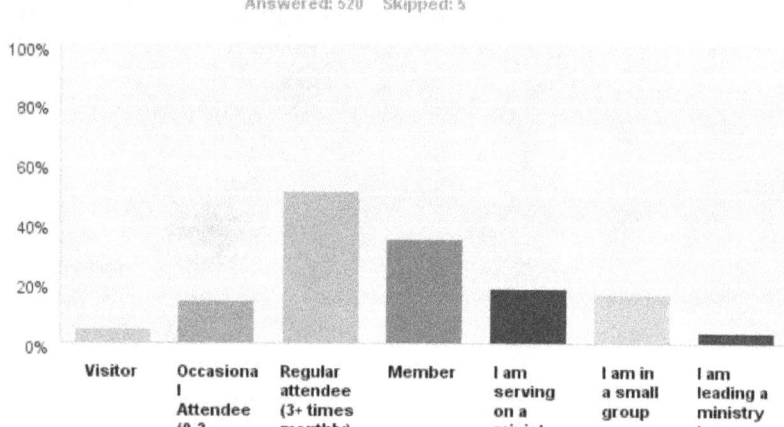

SUMMARY

It should be apparent from this discussion that those attending The Lighthouse are extremely diverse and mobile, which mirrors the diverse and transient nature of the surrounding community and the larger Port City metropolitan area. This makes The Lighthouse unique in that it is one of less than 6 percent of evangelical churches that can be classified as multi-ethnic in the United States. This poses both challenges and opportunities for The Lighthouse as it seeks to engage its ethnically dynamically context, which I will discuss more thoroughly in the chapters that follow.

2

The Lighthouse's Journey

Merging Attractional with Missional Ministry

OVER THE LAST SEVERAL years, The Lighthouse has been on a journey from a primarily attractional model of ministry—one focused on attracting people into the church building for a high-quality worship experience and programs to meet their needs—toward what they understand to be a missional model of ministry. Along the way, there have been course corrections, which have resulted in the church's current approach to ministry—an approach that I call mission-actional. I use this term to describe The Lighthouse's current mission praxis because, while their stated and understood goal is to become a missional church, their actual praxis reveals something else. Craig Van Gelder and Dwight Zscheile's evaluation of the development of the missional church discussion can shed some helpful light on what I mean by this.

THE MISSIONAL TREE

In their analysis of the missional church discussion that occurred over the preceding fifteen years, Van Gelder and Zscheile divide the plethora of past and current literature purporting to be missional into four branches of thought utilizing the analogy of a missional tree.[1] Each of the four branches—and their correlating sub-branches—represents a different view of the role agency within church life. In other words, the literature in each branch answers the question, "To what extent is God's agency operative

1. Van Gelder and Zscheile, *Missional Church*, 68–94.

and discernible within human choices?"[2] The first branch, discovering, places the emphasis of agency within the church and often within a single leader who can provide vision and strategy for those in the church to follow. This particular approach actually reaches back to traditional Western understandings that tend to separate "church" and "mission" and views missional as activities (ministries and other programs) that the church engages in within their community and beyond. As I will discuss later in this chapter, The Lighthouse currently resides in this branch and, more specifically, within the sub-branch, "Missional as Missions and Great Commission Obedience."[3] Revealing their self-understanding, however, they use the term missional to describe who they are and where they want to be.

While I will not elaborate on the second and third branches—utilizing and engaging—deeply here, I will briefly note that both demonstrate a clearer commitment to some of the core ideas of the original missional church discussion, while displaying a limited theological imagination in some way. For example, while those in the utilizing branch show some level of understanding and commitment to a Trinitarian view of the *missio Dei* and the importance of the Kingdom of God in relation to the church and the world, they tend to either overemphasize the focus of God's mission on individuals or minimize the role of the Spirit.[4] Similarly, those in the engaging branch also hold to the core theological ideas of the original discussion, while sometimes falling into the trap of providing a "how-to list" of things to do to become missional.[5]

The fourth branch, extending, seeks to remain faithful to the core ideas of the original discussion, while addressing some of the problems that arose. In taking this approach, those in this branch attempt to deepen the church's understanding of what it means to be missional, albeit with some variance among the three sub-branches contained within.[6] For example, as one seeking to bring a missional church understanding into conversation with a particular issue—multiethnic ministry—I tend to fall within the second sub-branch of this conversation with my research in The Lighthouse. What I share in common with others in this branch, however, is that I place primary agency with the Holy Spirit in a given

---

2. Van Gelder and Zscheile, *Missional Church*, 69.
3. Van Gelder and Zscheile, *Missional Church*, 70–74.
4. Van Gelder and Zscheile, *Missional Church*, 84.
5. Van Gelder and Zscheile, *Missional Church*, 90.
6. Van Gelder and Zscheile, *Missional Church*, 91.

context. As I stated earlier in my introduction, then, the primary task of those leading a local church becomes creating environments where the everyday people of God can discern and ultimately join the Spirit's initiatives in their context together as those sent into the world to partner with a God who is already on mission.[7] Missional, according to this view, then, speaks to identity, not simply activities.

In light of this understanding, throughout the rest of this chapter I will briefly narrate The Lighthouse's journey—a journey of re-discovery—of what it means to be a church on mission in a continually changing, ethnically diverse urban context. Within this narrative, I will highlight important events and decisions along the way that inform my analysis in the chapters to follow. As I do so, you will notice that I try to honor the way leadership at The Lighthouse understands and uses the term missional, which on occasion may seem contrary to my own understanding. I do this, however, to highlight some of the challenges that the church is facing on its journey toward becoming missional.

AN UNEXPECTED JOURNEY

Like many other churches in the Free Methodist tradition, The Lighthouse had humble beginnings. Launched as a Bible study in 1954, its first service was held in a school bus on the property it purchased to build a Free Methodist elementary school on Down Street in North Port City in 1957. Over the course of the next thirty-four years, several milestones were attained—a sanctuary was built in 1976 and expanded in 1988; the church grew and maintained an average attendance between thirty-five and one hundred; and in 1991, after an extended period of struggle and plateau, the congregation called Steve Walker to become their senior pastor. This watershed moment in the history of the church is where The Lighthouse's journey really took an exciting turn. While the preceding thirty-seven years of the church's journey were not uneventful, for the most part it seemed to be set on cruise control. Soon after Pastor Steve's hiring, however, the church changed its name to The Lighthouse and began a process of revitalization that resulted in steady growth. In 1994 the sanctuary was once again remodeled to hold more people so that the church could maintain its consistent trajectory of membership growth.[8]

---

7. Branson, "Ecclesiology and Leadership."

8. This history was provided in an interview with Pastor Walker in 2009, as well as The Lighthouse's website.

Charismatic Leadership and Missional Change

Course Correction #1: Worship with Jazz

During those early years under their charismatic new pastor, the church adopted an attractional model of ministry to reach its community. In other words, the church took an approach to ministry that depended on congregants inviting friends and neighbors to a Sunday service that was high in quality and professional. Services consisted of a high-energy worship experience led by professional jazz musicians and relevant biblical messages targeting the felt needs of attendees delivered with passion and energy—a format that continues to this day. This model of ministry suited their new pastor's gifts and capitalized on the musical talents of their members, resulting in immediate steady growth.

An unexpected drawback of this shift in ministry philosophy, however, is that it laid the foundation for an adaptive challenge that the church would face over a decade later, when Pastor Steve began to lead the church toward a new mission focus in the community—over-dependence on the charismatic leader. By placing such a heavy focus on the experience on the Sunday-experience, the focus shifted heavily to a church-centered approach to mission emphasizing the church as the center of God's activity.[9] In this model, Pastor Steve became the person most responsible for producing a high-quality experience for the religious consumers who came through the doors. This ultimately helped to reinforce a clergy-centered ministry schema that is still shaping the theological imagination of congregants and staff today. Pastor Steve acknowledged his influence and alluded to the salience of this clergy-centered schema during one of our interviews, when he stated plainly that, "This is very much a pastor-led church . . . everyone does not have an equal voice with me." I will discuss the evidence for this claim further in chapter 4.

As the church continued to grow, it ran into a more immediate and practical dilemma; it had no further room to expand. Rising real estate costs in Port City made buying a larger property an unrealistic proposition for the growing but not overly affluent urban church. Further, the property could not handle further expansion due to parking shortages and the space needs of the school. At this point, the church was faced with an adaptive challenge that would require Pastor Steve, the staff, and the entire congregation to learn new values and practices if it was to continue on its trajectory toward growth and increased impact on its community. As a result,

---

9. Roxburgh, *Joining God*.

The Lighthouse's Journey

Pastor Steve, Ella (his wife), and their inner-circle of prayer partners began praying for a solution to their space issues. According to Pastor Steve:

> We weren't sure what to do. We couldn't buy a larger property, and we didn't have the room or the money to do significant expansion on our current property. We also knew that God didn't want us to become complacent and stop trying to reach people for the Kingdom, so we were at a loss. We were at a crossroads that drove me to my knees to seek God's direction for the future of our ministry.

Not long after, the answer would come to Pastor Steve. If the church couldn't expand where it was . . . it would multiply.

Course Correction #2: Following the River

After hearing from the Lord early in 1999 through a series of conversations with colleagues in other congregations and some books he had been reading, Pastor Steve became excited about the potential of church planting as a way to expand The Lighthouse's influence and reach the city. He began casting vision to his ministry staff and leaders for a new model of ministry—a multiplication approach that would come to be known as The River Church. After a time of discussion and prayer, the church adopted this new approach and adjusted its ministry model. At the heart of this new approach was the vision for The Lighthouse to plant a church in each of Port City's nine council districts by the year 2010—an effort that would come to be known as Mission 2010. This new focus coincided with a renewed emphasis on church planting within the conference of churches The Lighthouse belongs to. What followed was an unprecedented time of ministry fruitfulness in the history of the church.

The church proceeded to plant thirty-five churches through the time of my interviews with Pastor Steve—both locally and globally—as it embraced its new focus over the next ten years. According to Pastor Steve, The Lighthouse planted ten churches in Port City and in neighboring cities, two more in other parts of the United States, and more than twenty internationally. Twelve of these international plants occurred in Ethiopia through partnership with Free Methodist World Missions, and the rest occurred in three nations where some of The Lighthouse's new congregants came from—five in the Philippines, two in Indonesia, and one in Kenya. While not all of these churches ultimately survived, the new focus on church multiplication caught on with the congregation and expanded beyond Pastor Steve's

Charismatic Leadership and Missional Change

original vision for Port City. Interestingly, this apparent success created some mixed emotions for Pastor Steve, who realized as 2010 drew closer that they were not going to reach their original goal of planting a church in each of Port City's nine council districts. In one of my many conversations with him, he recalled:

> As we got closer and closer to the end of Mission 2010, I spent quite a bit of time worrying that we weren't going to reach our originally stated goal in Mission 2010—to plant a church in all nine council districts in Port City. I wondered what that might do to the congregation's morale. As I reflected on what we had accomplished, however, I began to realize that God had actually done much more. I mean, we funded, partnered, or sent teams out to plant thirty-five churches! Wow! How incredible is that?

Incredible indeed. More incredible, however, was that in the midst of The Lighthouse's efforts at living out its river church identity, the winds of change began to blow again. Only this time, the changes God intended for The Lighthouse would push against the church and clergy-centric ministry schemas that had been shaping the church's mission praxis for more than a decade.

Course Correction #3: The River Flows Toward Mission-Actional

In 2005 Pastor Ella began a Doctor of Ministry program at Fuller Seminary that would challenge her and, ultimately, Pastor Steve in ways they did not expect. When I asked her to define what it meant for the church to be on mission, she noted:

> Before 2005, I couldn't have answered that question. I was only familiar with a church model of doing ministry—attractional. The Fuller DMin introduced me to the concept of missional. I began to see mission as we need to go out and be a blessing to the community. We are on mission when we reach out practically—food, needs, context-based, etc. This experience re-directed my entire thought process about what it meant for the church to be on mission in its community.

During her early time at Fuller, authors like Reggie McNeal and Alan Hirsch began to reshape Pastor Ella's ministry schema in some significant ways. Accordingly, it did not take long for her to introduce her new learning to her husband. According to Pastor Ella:

> Reggie McNeal's *Present Future* was huge in my thinking. I brought this to Steve, the small group leaders—at the time I was overseeing small groups—and Halogen leaders. We were in the midst of planning Halogen.[10] Then Steve took it to the staff and the Leadership Council. . . . Alan Hirsch's *The Shaping of Things to Come and Forgotten Ways* were also very formative for Steve and me. I was doing a lot of different reading on the topic. Much of my focus became what it could look like for our church to develop a missional DNA.

Around the time Pastor Steve was being introduced to the concepts of the missional church by Pastor Ella, he was also invited to attend an Externally Focused Church Conference in Denver by local Port City leader Errol Marks. According to Pastor Steve, this experience watered the missional church seeds that had been planted in him by Pastor Ella and the books she had recommended to him. As God continued to redefine their ministry schema in new ways, he and Ella began talking about their new missional learning with the Ministry Staff Leaders, and together, they began talking and praying consistently about how God might want them to reach their immediate community. Not long after, The Lighthouse's journey toward becoming more engaged with diverse expressions of mission in their community would begin, accelerated by what would turn out to be a divine opportunity. The church was presented with the chance to buy the building next door to expand their facilities and focus their efforts toward a more outward expression of ministry in their community.

This phase of The Lighthouse's journey is revealing, highlighting some important issues that I will briefly introduce here. First, the influence of *Externally Focused Church*[11] on Pastor Steve's thought process and the focus on purchasing the building to offer ministries to the community reveals his and the staff's emphasis on initiating and engaging in mission activities in the community. There is little reflection or adjustment in their current church-centered activities; instead, we see a move toward increasing activity outside their walls on top of their current initiatives. As I discussed earlier in this chapter, this presents the picture of a church that is squarely

---

10. Halogen is a church plant that began as an alternative service on Sunday evenings to reach young adults. Although it still meets on the property, it is now an independent church in the Free Methodist Church Southern California.

11. Rusaw and Swanson, *Externally Focused.*

Charismatic Leadership and Missional Change

in the first branch of Van Gelder and Zscheile's missional tree. The shift in their mission praxis is not so much heading toward missional as it is a return to older paradigms of ecclesio-centric mission emphasizing outreach in the community as the pastor indicated.

The second issue reinforces this understanding, as the discernment and decision-making process at the church centers heavily around the paid professionals with no interaction (that I observed or was told about) with their neighbors. Instead, Pastor Ella's education, the books she and Pastor Steve are reading together, and the discussions and prayer with the other paid pastoral staff are driving their discernment and decision-making process. This serves as a practical demonstration of a clergy-centered, top-down leadership schema that shapes The Lighthouse's mission praxis. It also informs a third issue. The Lighthouse's mission praxis is heavily focused on engaging in mission activities "for," rather than "with" their community. This highlights a tendency among many in the staff to treat their neighbors as objects instead of subjects in their mission activities. I will elaborate more on these ideas in the following chapters. First, however, I will briefly narrate the rest of The Lighthouse's shift toward a mission-actional posture in their community.

TAKING THE EXPRESSWAY TO MISSION-ACTIONAL: THE LIGHTHOUSE COMMUNITY CENTER

Pastor Steve was pleasantly surprised when he received an unexpected offer from Red, the owner of the electrical business next door to the church offices, in 2006. "Would you like to buy my building Steve? I'm retiring and am willing to sell it to you under market value in a private sale."[12] Pastor Steve was shocked, but excited, and after securing support from the staff and approval from the leadership council, he led the church forward in its purchase of the first property adjacent to the church to come up for sale in years. Initially, however, the staff wasn't sure how they would use the building specifically. Some of the staff and leadership council wanted to use it to expand current church purposes as a place for small groups to meet, as new office space, or even as a place to hold large events. It became clear through the process, however, that they would use the building to somehow carry out the "Reach" part of the church's mission statement—Reach, Teach, Mend, Send. Making too much business and ministry sense to pass up, they

12. Interview with Pastor Walker in 2010.

accepted Red's offer and purchased the property for $648,000. While this was a financial stretch for the church, it was an investment that showed everyone involved where the church was heading in its local mission focus.

Little did Pastors Steve and Ella, the ministry staff, and the leadership council know how profoundly this move would affect The Lighthouse. According to Pastor Steve, around the time of the purchase:

> The major emphasis on local church planting had begun to slow. We were still doing a lot planting overseas, but we had been praying about our one-mile radius for about a year . . . and Ella and I were both being prompted through prayer about what we were doing in our neighborhood. So, we began empowering Paul and Tina with IC Kidz more and raising awareness among our church about our community needs, and we brought on Xavier to reach out to our Hispanic neighbors. By the time the community center came along, the church was ready.

The building—and idea—that would soon become known as The Lighthouse Community Center energized the congregation. The leaders and congregants alike had been praying about how to influence their community for some time, and now it seemed that the answer had come. The building would be used to impact the one-mile radius around the church. An intercultural taskforce of missions-minded lay leaders was put together and led by the executive pastor, and together, this group began to investigate how the fledgling community center should be used. As a part of this process, they designed and administered a community survey door-to-door with several community residents and brainstormed ideas that they felt would meet community needs.

Together, these efforts represented another significant shift in the mission praxis of the church. This was the first intentional effort I uncovered in my research where pastoral leadership established a construction site where diverse voices could be included in the discernment and decision-making processes of the church. My research also revealed that the church had never previously sought intentional input from their neighbors relating to their mission practices. These unprecedented moves by leadership represented a first attempt to shift discernment and decision-making away from the paid ministry staff, the current center of power in the church. The potential benefit from these efforts would be mitigated by the actions of the associate pastor assigned to lead the taskforce—Pastor Peter[13]—however, as he struggled

---

13. See Appendix A for a coded list of interview participants.

with implementing this new approach in light of the existing top-down, clergy-centered leadership schema that was informing his own leadership practices. I will elaborate on this more in chapters 3 and 4.

In the meantime, positive developments around the community center continued as the taskforce engaged its process. Pastor Steve spearheaded a drive to raise $120,000 in November that year to renovate the building, and he accomplished that goal primarily by vision casting and appeals to the congregation on Sundays. A part-time director for the center was hired to develop programs, form partnerships, raise funds, and mobilize congregants for service in the new center. Energy and excitement for this new vehicle of community transformation was reaching a fervor pitch.

Not So Fast: An Unexpected Detour

Plans for the community center were suddenly derailed, however, when the city offices placed a stop work order on the center over zoning issues in the summer of 2007. What ensued was a three-year ordeal that finally concluded in the summer of 2010 with the church being granted the zoning permits it needed to move forward with its plans. In the meantime, the three-year period of inactivity around the building seemingly derailed whatever momentum had been gained through those early victories.

Two of my interview respondents mentioned how demoralizing it was for many in the church the longer the process dragged on. For example, Betty, a lay leader in the church, said, "There seemed to be a lot of growing frustration among people. People were increasingly asking what was happening. We just weren't hearing anything from the staff." According to Pastor Peter, however, this seeming derailment of the church's dream for the community center may have actually set the church on a healthier course toward cultivating a missional DNA in the congregation.

> The events began a big turning point. The setbacks we experienced gave us time and helped us develop outreach on our own without a building. Otherwise, we could have had a place to simply throw money at. It forced us to keep pushing for missional change with the result that we have seen many more initiatives begin that may have otherwise not happened.

While there was certainly some frustration voiced by some of the interview respondents regarding how the whole scenario had unfolded, most seemed to agree with this assessment implicitly as they shared stories of new mission initiatives that emerged during the three-year stoppage. Some of these initiatives included conducting a basketball tournament for kids in the neighborhood, holding fitness classes for the community, and hosting a Girl Scouts troupe. According to Pastor Peter, some of the most valuable and enduring initiatives were a result of passengers picked up along the journey, however.

Re-routing... But with New Traveling Companions

This circumstantial detour motivated Pastor Steve and some of the pastoral staff to reevaluate their options in light of this unexpected development. In conversation with the community center director and Pastor Dave, Pastor Steve made the decision to actively pursue new partnerships with individuals, groups, and agencies that might produce programs that could ultimately be housed in the community center. As Pastor Steve guided this change of course on The Lighthouse's journey toward mission-actional, it represented another shift in his and, ultimately, the church's mission schema. Until then, the church understood that participation in God's mission should be expressed primarily through proclamation and acts of compassion (like their food pantry). Their new mission focus moving forward, however, would be more holistic in nature and emphasize partnerships.

This shift in ministry philosophy is important to note here, as the emerging mission-actional ministry schema clearly begins to shape the mission practices of the church over the next two years. As Pastor Steve and the pastoral staff become more and more invested in this new mission focus in the community, for example, the church formed key partnerships with several individuals and agencies outside of the church without the use of the building. Some of the more significant partnerships were formed with: (1) Mark Smalls, a former NFL linebacker and entrepreneur, who started a charter school on the campus—the Micro Enterprise Charter Academy (MECA); (2) Marv Stevens, a local Christian entrepreneur, who offered a computer-based graphic arts training program for youth in a temporary computer lab set up in one of the other buildings; and (3) the Port City municipal office. Through this partnership, The Lighthouse was able to offer disaster preparedness seminars, neighborhood beautification projects, and community fairs, and began to explore how it might offer leadership training and computer courses for nearby low-income residents. Through another agency, the church began to explore how it might house a Family Intervention and Referral Program, while further

Charismatic Leadership and Missional Change

partnerships resulted in exploring the possibility of such varied programs as fitness classes and a Girl Scouts troop. Some of the church's own efforts included sponsoring a basketball tournament for kids in the neighborhood and a community garden, which since has expanded to multiple locations and offers fresh produce for both church members and community residents alike. While it is impossible to tell from my observations or the interview data whether these types of programs would have been foreign thinking for the majority of the staff and congregants before the building was purchased, it seems like a reasonable deduction due to the absence of such programs prior to the building purchase.

As reports of these new initiatives began to disseminate through the congregation, people began to see what was missionally possible without the community center while they waited for the zoning issue with the city to work itself out. Over the next few years, the leadership of The Lighthouse continued to cultivate mission-actional DNA among the congregation through new events and initiatives such as: (1) Serve the City, a one-day annual effort that mobilizes service teams from several local churches to do acts of service in the community; (2) Bible Fiesta Fun, the church's annual vacation bible school for kids that was moved to a local park in an attempt to attract more neighborhood children; (3) other large events that the church has sponsored outside the walls for several years; and (4) through continual vision casting and promotion by Pastor Steve and the rest of the staff. One example of this effort was "Heroes of the Faith," a web-based contest that had congregants nominate others in the congregation for being involved in creative missional ministries outside of the walls of the church.

Although these events appeared to produce little fruit in the sense of conversions or long-term sustainable community transformation, they did seem to contribute toward the ongoing shift toward an external mission focus in the community as people's schemas of what it meant to be a church on mission were continually challenged. For example, Sandra, one of the ministry staff leaders who was involved in one of these events, said that, "The church hasn't really seen any fruit from it . . . but it reinforced them coming. . . . We used about fifty volunteers from the church while we were there." Similarly, Pastor Steve said that while "CWOW[14] is not really great evangelistically . . . it is very effective for communicating that we will get out of the box

---

14. Church Without Walls (CWOW) is an annual Sunday worship service held in a park up the street from the church in place of the regular Sunday service.

for our neighborhood. . . . We did receive fifty-five information cards from boxes of food we gave out though, so we can follow-up with them."

These comments are revealing, as they demonstrate an awareness at some level on the part of leadership that the new mission efforts of the church are producing mixed results. They are not seeing conversions or tangible change in the community as a result of their efforts, yet some congregants' practices are changing due to the emphasis on events and service projects in the community. Even here, however, results are less than hoped for, as Pastor Steve admits that he has "mixed feelings about CWOW . . . because I wish more of our people would come." This admission acknowledges at some level that the church's mission activities in the community are still driven primarily by leadership with a low level of ownership by many congregants. When combined with the statements above, it also reveals that many in leadership feel good that they are doing activities in the neighborhood and providing services within the church that they perceive to be helpful for the community. Ultimately, this demonstrates an ongoing commitment to an ecclesio-centric and leader-heavy approach that may be interfering with the church's desire and ability to engage their community in meaningful ways. I will delve more deeply into this issue in chapters 4 and 5.

Back on Course: The Community Center Opens

While the amount of mission activities inside and outside of the church continued to increase during the three-year period between 2007 and 2010, the church finally saw its patience pay off in June 2010 when the community center opened its doors to the public. This milestone was exciting for church members and provided more fuel for the mission-actional DNA that was being cultivated while the building's future was uncertain. Church leadership immediately began a drop-in center for at-risk youth in the community that is open five days a week. Shortly thereafter, the church funded and began to develop a life-skills class for community residents. Under Pastor Ella's leadership, the church also launched a community garden on the church's campus that has since been duplicated into a second location in a nearby city park.

These programs were just the beginning, however, as church leadership continued to forge ahead in its journey with its new traveling companions. Over the final year of my research, for example, the church continued to cultivate its relationship with the Port City municipal office by exploring how it might offer leadership training and computer courses for nearby low-income residents. Concurrently, it also sought out new partnerships, such as discerning with another agency whether the new community center could house a family intervention and referral program or if they could provide entrepreneurial training in micro-enterprise for at-risk youth with the support of the Bank of America. Collectively, these efforts demonstrated church leadership's commitment to continue moving forward on its journey toward mission-actional with new traveling companions as well as its willingness to re-discover itself along the way.

These efforts also further highlight the nature of the mission schema emerging at The Lighthouse. First, discernment and decision-making for the church's mission activities center strongly with pastoral leadership, away from the margins of church and community life. This is demonstrated by the fact that the overwhelming majority of these initiatives and potential partnerships were being explored by pastoral staff, not congregants. Second, the proliferation of mission activities that are emerging continue to reveal the ecclesio-centric understanding of the locus of God's mission activities held by pastoral leadership and many in the congregation. Most of these initiatives and partnerships are intended to occur within the confines of church space rather than in the community. Those that do occur in the community are either existing church programs that are temporarily transplanted in the community, like Bible Fiesta Fun, or are run by the church for the community (the community garden). Third, while the increased focus on forming partnerships with others in the community is a positive development on one level, the continued emphasis on providing services for the community continues to objectify their neighbors rather than humanize them on another level. Again, I will expand on these issues moving forward over the next two chapters.

SUMMARY

In this chapter I have briefly highlighted the key decisions and events that have facilitated The Lighthouse's journey toward merging attractional with a mission-actional expression of ministry in its community. While its journey is far from over, I have demonstrated that it has been characterized by unexpected detours and course corrections that have begun to reshape the church's mission schema. As this new schema has taken root in the pastoral staff's theological imagination, it has begun to reshape the way they perceive the nature of God's mission in the world and The Lighthouse's role in it. The result has been an emerging mission praxis that is more focused on providing services for the community through partnerships and other external mission activities that meet perceived needs. In the next chapter, I will discuss more in depth how leadership has facilitated this journey by examining the primary resources utilized to drive mission-actional change in the church.

3

Leadership Resources Driving Change at The Lighthouse

FOR A CHANGE PROCESS to be successful, leaders need to effectively utilize the resources available to them. As revealed through my research, Pastor Steve and the other ministry leaders consistently utilized two primary resources to drive the change process toward mission-actional ministry at The Lighthouse. The first is the charismatic leadership model utilized by Pastor Steve to influence his followers. The second is a missional theology of place that Pastor Steve and other leaders are constructing that has refocused the church's mission efforts toward their surrounding community. As we will discover through the discussion in the rest of this chapter, the utilization of these two resources speaks not just to the issue of how but also why Pastor Steve and the pastoral leadership team are leading missional change at The Lighthouse the way they are. We will also begin to see how utilizing these resources the way they have has contributed toward some adaptive challenges at The Lighthouse.

CHARISMATIC LEADERSHIP AT THE LIGHTHOUSE

According to Jay Conger and Rabindra Kanungo, charismatic leaders are those whose followers attribute special characteristics to them because of their ability to: (1) identify and connect environmental constraints and opportunities for the organization with their followers' needs and abilities; (2) discern and communicate a powerful vision that resonates with their followers; and (3) influence and deploy followers in pursuit of that vision.[1]

---

1. Conger and Kanungo, *Charismatic Leadership*, 49.

Consequently, charisma is attributed to a leader by followers who strongly identify with that leader and believe that he or she possesses special qualities. According to the data generated through my research, Pastor Steve's leadership style fits this definition very well.

As you can see from some of the words and phrases that I have italicized in comments from my interview respondents, Pastor Steve has several positive leadership indicators that identify him with Conger and Kanungo's charismatic leadership paradigm.

TABLE 1

PASTOR STEVE'S POSITIVE LEADERSHIP INDICATORS

P4—"Steve is someone with *vision* and *gets the team to buy in*. His greatest strength is positivity. He believes we can do it!"	L2—"Steve *places people in positions that maximize their skills and strengths*. He has non-stop ideas and then is on to the next thing. He takes input, but makes the hard decisions. He usually vets ideas pretty thoroughly before bringing them to the group."	L4—"Steve is a top-down, *charismatic leader* who is personality-based. He carries *vision*. If he has it, people follow it . . . great energy and enthusiasm. He is a dynamic leader."
P6—"He is open, not closed off, to any idea that is missional. He will hear it out. Steve really believes in people. He doesn't put people in molds, but really hones in on their uniqueness. He really believes they can do a good job."	L5—"Steve's leadership style is very *visionary* . . . *charismatic, he can sway people*."	P7—"He operates with wisdom and there are boundaries, but not restrictive at all. People feel comfortable around him."
P3—"Steve is a cheerleader, an *encourager, empowering, but very strong and visionary leader*, entrepreneurial, positive, believes in people."	L3—"Steve is gifted at pushing everyone a little bit at a time, small steps. He doesn't push too hard, but pushes with wisdom. He is balanced, tactful, challenging, and *resonating*."	P8—"Steve is a *big picture guy*; an intellectual leader who puts ideas out there hoping others will pick up on them. He is silently aggressive in a good way."

He is visionary, can get people to buy into that vision, places people where they can flourish in their strengths in pursuit of that vision, is positive and encouraging, and resonates with his followers. Overall, he is a highly respected, loved, and admired leader who has done an amazing job of turning a church around in a city with a very difficult spiritual climate and in a specific community that has continued to change and shift demographically during his entire tenure.

Shifting from Top-Down to Team-Based Leadership

His ability to inspire the congregants at The Lighthouse has served both Pastor Steve and the church well since he came to the church in 1991. From the data I collected, it becomes clear in fact that Pastor Steve's ability to discern and cast vision, rally people around that vision, and mobilize people to pursue that vision is one of the most valuable leadership resources he has at his disposal. It is not a stretch to suggest that it is the reason that he and the church are on a journey toward mission-actional together. He will be the first to tell you that he is not perfect, however. He acknowledged to me on several occasions during the course of my research that he needs to adjust his leadership style to keep up with changes in the church, the culture, and the context, but that he has struggled to do so. As I will demonstrate briefly here but elaborate more in depth in chapter 4, this appears to be an adaptive challenge that Pastor Steve is facing due to the leadership schema shaping his values and practice—a top-down, charismatic schema that centers agency for missional change in the leader.

According to Pastor Steve, there are three significant issues that contributed to this realization. First, for the first time during his tenure at The Lighthouse, the church had experienced some plateau and seeming stagnation that he couldn't seem to fix. This plateau lasted several years—from 2005 to 2009—and seemed to relate to the Downey church plant that saw one hundred Anglo members leave as part of the team late in 2005. This "white flight," as he called it, contributed toward a demographic shift in the church that helped it to better reflect the ethnic diversity in the neighborhood. Yet, it also contributed toward some financial problems for the church, as those who left with the team constituted a significant percentage of the giving base. Pastor Steve's inability to figure out a solution for the first time in his pastorate began to wear on him, and it caused him to begin thinking about the necessity of a new way of leading.

The second issue was the realization that the culture had been moving to a more team-based mentality, and his top-down approach "might not resonate as much with the younger generation."[2] Third, he acknowledged in one of our interviews that his single greatest inhibitor is leadership multiplication. He realized that if he couldn't raise the leadership base in the church, it was going to become increasingly difficult to do ministry in the community. Consequently, he expressed a desire to become more team-based instead of top-down.

The data suggests that this desire to shed the top-down approach for a team-based one is needed as well. Many of the negative leadership indicators communicated by the lay leader respondents in interviews seemed to speak directly to this issue. One respondent actually used the phrase "top-down" to describe Pastor Steve's leadership style, suggesting that if "Steve doesn't buy in to the decision or idea, it isn't going to happen."[3] Three of the respondents agreed with one another, suggesting that Pastor Steve "often seems to have an idea processed and thought out, and had his mind made up coming into a meeting."[4] Unless there is significant pushback from someone in the leadership council, "he almost always gets his way," said another.[5] Two of these respondents indicated that there was a feeling of de-valuing because of these experiences on the leadership council, and that it took away some of their motivation to serve.

An email Pastor Steve sent in January 2010 to his newly forming executive team seems to explain both Steve's and the respondents' desires for team-based ministry well. With a good level of self-awareness, Pastor Steve presented a diagram that portrayed this challenge and his goals for creating a new leadership culture.

TABLE 2

THE FIVE LEADERSHIP BOXES

Autocratic decision by leader	Leader proposes decision, listens to feedback, then decides	Team proposes decision, leader has final decision	Joint decision with team as equals	Full delegation of decision to team

In his email, he identifies his current operating matrix for decisions and also where he would like to be. To his executive team he says:

2. Interview with Pastor Steve in 2010.
3. Interview with L4 in 2009.
4. Interview with L4 in 2009.
5. Interview with L2 in 2009.

Charismatic Leadership and Missional Change

> Until we get the identity and activity of the executive team more clearly defined and operational, we will be in a bit of a hybrid model of the past and the future. The past meaning I move things forward as a leader with input from the team, and the future meaning team thinking that makes decisions together. . . . I am working towards the middle box. We are probably in Box 2 right now. It really depends on the issue. . . . Some issues we are in box 1, some issues we are in Box 5. . . . Part of the issue is deciding what issues the executive team takes up.

In my observations and experience with Pastor Steve over the past several years, Steve's self-analysis is correct. As a top-down, charismatic leader, he tends to propose decisions and/or solutions, gather some feedback, and then make the decision a majority of the time. He has often assessed the situation in advance, coming into a meeting with his mind seemingly made up. While this approach has often served him well, it can also create challenges for a charismatic leader. According to Conger and Kanungo, the longer a leader stays in an organization, the more likely he or she is to rely on old data when making environmental assessments in decision-making. This raises the chance that the leader coming in with his or her mind made up will make the wrong decision for the situation, putting the organization in a precarious place. This problem often stems from over-dependence on the charismatic leader, an issue created by the heroic leader complex often bought into by leader and followers alike. At The Lighthouse, this issue of over-dependence on the leader appears to be an adaptive challenge resulting from Pastor Steve's charismatic leadership style.

We see in this instance, then, that Pastor Steve's greatest resource in the missional change process also has the potential to be an inhibitor. Pastor Steve's inability to shift his leadership to more of a team-based decision-making style as the context and culture shifts around him is hindered by the primary schema informing his approach toward leadership—a top-down, charismatic leadership schema. This schema has shaped an adaptive challenge that he has struggled to overcome in his personal leadership, which has ultimately contributed toward a more significant adaptive challenge faced by the entire congregation—over-dependence on the charismatic leader. In this instance, then, the resources that have served him best in the past—qualities and traits associated with charismatic leadership and influence—might actually be holding the church back in some ways on its journey toward missional. In fact, I suggest that a primary reason the church is engaging in mission-actional ministry rather than a missional expression

CONSTRUCTING A MISSIONAL THEOLOGY OF PLACE AT THE LIGHTHOUSE

closer to their original goal relates directly to his leadership style. I will elaborate on this more deeply in chapter 4.

A second resource that Pastor Steve and the leadership of The Lighthouse have been utilizing to drive the change process in the church is an emerging mission theology that they have been constructing within the congregation. Though multifaceted, I refer to this new mission theology as a missional theology of place, which reflects the heavy emphasis Pastor Steve, the pastoral staff, and many in the congregation are placing on impacting people within the one-mile radius surrounding the church with the gospel. Before discussing the nature of this mission theology and the means Pastor Steve and the staff are using to construct it within the congregation, however, I will first elaborate on how I am using the term "place" here as well as the placeless-ness characterizing American society at large that impinges upon The Lighthouse in its context.

Place as Culture Construction, Shared Memory, and Lived Experience

Many view place today simply as a way of describing a specific location—akin to a container—where life and social interactions occur.[6] This is understandable, as the concept of place certainly carries with it an aspect of geographical location where life occurs. Neglected in this simplistic understanding, however, is place's role in shaping human meanings, memories, and experience. When we lose this understanding, we are left with the idea that certain phenomena can happen just as easily and certainly in one place as in another.[7]

This line of thinking is a result of the universalizing tendencies of modernity, however, and has been refuted by scholars spanning such diverse disciplines as anthropology,[8] geography,[9] and philosophy.[10] These scholars assert people and places are not the same everywhere, suggesting that

---

6. Rodman, "Empowering Place," 204.
7. Inge, *Christian Theology of Place*, 5.
8. See Feld and Basso, *Senses of Place*; Low and Lawrence-Zuniga, *Space and Place*.
9. See Soja, *Postmodern Geographies*.
10. See Casey, *Fate of Place*; Heidegger, "Building Dwelling Thinking."

places are complex social constructions that bring together social history, selective memory, and personal and social experience to link people from a given locale together into a shared history and identity.[11] Distinct places are in fact unique, carrying within them meanings fashioned as much by the people inhabiting a particular place as the place itself. Places, then, are not simply geographical containers; rather, they are inherently relational locations where culture construction, shared memory, and lived experience occur. This makes differentiating a place from the community/communities associated with it an impossible task.[12]

Losing Our Place

While this phenomenological understanding of place is being recaptured in the academy today, numerous scholars have argued convincingly that one of the consequences of modernity has been the deconstruction and devaluing of place in Western society.[13] They attribute this cultural phenomenon to several factors: (1) the rise of space and time; (2) the development of new technologies that have given us unprecedented access to places around the globe; (3) the impact of globalization that has resulted in unprecedented migration during the twentieth and twenty-first centuries; and (4) American capitalist values relating to the pursuit of wealth and success that inform mobility.[14] Together, these factors have contributed toward a significant adaptive challenge: an increasing sense of "placeless-ness"—or lack of meaningful attachment to home and place—experienced among rising numbers of people in American society.[15]

As this placeless-ness has permeated American society, the challenge has become twofold for local churches throughout America's cities, which are most directly impacted by this phenomenon. First, churches have to figure out how to minister in neighborhoods that are in constant flux. But second, many churches are themselves being shaped by the very sociocultural factors that are shaping their surrounding communities. As such, many local churches face a serious adaptive challenge in their congregational life and mission praxis. They have also become placeless,

11. Kahn, "Your Place and Mine," 167–68.
12. Inge, *Christian Theology of Place*, 26, 124–25.
13. See Casey, *Fate of Place*; Inge, *Christian Theology of Place*; Bouma-Prediger and Walsh, *Beyond Homelessness*.
14. Hendrickson, "Displacement," 106–7.
15. Bouma-Prediger and Walsh, *Beyond Homelessness*.

maintaining little more than a physical presence in their communities, while members commute in from the suburbs or other neighborhoods they are living in. Consequently, many local churches continue to function as commuter churches, as their members drive in on Sundays to consume religious goods and services.[16] As this occurs, it is challenging for members to remain or, in some cases, become meaningfully connected to people in the community immediately surrounding their church. The church building then primarily becomes a place where church members have meaningful interactions with one another on Sundays, while remaining detached from the surrounding community the rest of the week. Unfortunately, this often leads to decline unless the church is able to remain large enough and continues to offer enough meaningful programs and services to draw in people from a regional constituency.[17]

The Lighthouse Rediscovering Its Place

In its recent history, The Lighthouse has also been affected by this adaptive challenge of placeless-ness. Like many other large and growing multiethnic churches, The Lighthouse has drawn from a regional rather than a primarily local constituency over the years.[18] As I detailed in chapter 2, however, this has begun to change over the last decade as Pastor Steve and the staff have continued to move The Lighthouse toward mission-actional ministry. The church is now more embedded in its local context, both through its programming as well as through the congregants who call The Lighthouse home. Just under half (46.3 percent) of the respondents have been attending the church for three years or less, for example, and 43.9 percent now live within three miles of the church campus. While there have been several contributing factors toward this transformation, the primary impetus behind this change (as mentioned earlier) has been the missional theology of place that Pastors Steve and Ella and the rest of the pastoral staff have been embedding within the congregation. In the rest of this chapter, I will discuss: (1) the nature of this mission theology; (2) how Pastor Steve and the pastoral staff have gone about constructing this mission theology in the congregation; and (3) how deeply this mission theology is embedded within the congregation. This will shed some light on how Pastor Steve and

---

16. Branson and Martinez, *Churches, Cultures, and Leadership.*
17. Hendrickson, "Displacement," 117.
18. See DeYoung et al., *United by Faith*; Emerson, *People of the Dream.*

the staff are attempting to transform the cultural schema informing this adaptive challenge.

COMMITTING TO ITS COMMUNITY THROUGH HOLISTIC MISSION

During my first interview with Pastor Steve, he was quick to tell me that The Lighthouse has had the same mission statement for the last fifteen years: Reach unchurched people, Teach believers to love Jesus, Mend broken lives, and Send disciples into ministry. But he also acknowledged the way The Lighthouse is attempting to live out that mission has changed dramatically over the past decade. My interviews with pastoral staff and key lay leaders, the survey I administered to the congregation, and my personal observations all confirm this shift in ministry philosophy from a primarily attractional approach—centered on inviting people into a high-production, high energy Sunday worship service where people can hear and respond to the Gospel—to the current mission-actional one focusing on its immediate community.

Twelve out of thirteen interview respondents each discussed in some way how The Lighthouse's mission priority has been shifting to its immediate community over the past few years. For example, Lynette—one of the ministry staff leaders—noted:

> Mission 2010 was catalytic for a bigger heart for Long Beach. After five years, it felt like we began moving toward what I felt the church and our focus should be.... Our heart continued to grow for our immediate neighborhood. We began loving Andy Street intentionally, and engaged in programs like Serve the City.

Likewise, Leroy—one of the lay leader respondents—shared how much the church has changed racially since officially joining as a member (sometime in 1999 or 2000) and how excited he is by the church's new focus on reaching the surrounding community through the community center. He shared that, "It's been really rewarding getting to know the residents of Andy Street, interacting with them, and identifying some of their needs. I'm excited to see what programs we develop out of this."

Several other respondents shared this excitement, expressing further appreciation for how The Lighthouse has supported the work of programs like IC Kidz, which serves local kids in the community with remote afterschool Bible clubs and activities, Serve the City, and CWOW.

Similarly, Sandra and Leroy highlighted several ways that programming in The Lighthouse's children's ministry has moved its focus away from church-centered to community-focused over the years, such as moving its annual vacation bible school up the street to Reyes Park and renaming it Bible Fiesta Fun, conducting three to four outreaches per year in the park, and hosting an annual Halloween party in the parking lot for kids in the community called Trunk or Treat.

While these events are just a sample of how the leadership of The Lighthouse has shifted its mission focus to the surrounding community, they also reflect something else: Pastor Steve's bias toward events over process to engage the community. In a follow-up interview I conducted with him, he acknowledged this bias, stating:

> The only example I can think of is the tension point between ends of the spectrum—I wouldn't go as far as you (the researcher) with attractional versus missional or relational. Part of it is my sense of responsibility that I feel financially: Will missional give us the dollars we need to sustain our staff and operations that won't affect our bottom line? That's where the tension is. I love the emphasis on missional and have heartily embraced that, but I feel the tension when we start going that way. The other part of that is I'm probably still more crisis/event evangelism than you are. You are more slow and process oriented. The tension here is from my desire to see numerical growth, more results quicker, especially conversions.

Pastor Steve reveals his ecclesio-centric motivation here for encouraging his staff to stage these types of one-time events in the community. His main priority is to see the church grow, which shapes his preferred approach to outreach in the community. He concurrently feels the need to ensure the financial viability of the church moving forward, which helps to reinforce the event-driven, attractional approach that plays to his strengths as a charismatic leader and evangelist, and that he believes can produce quicker results. These concerns for growing and sustaining the church drive Pastor Steve toward approaches that tend to treat people as objects of mission rather than as subjects and co-participants in God's mission. Relationships with their neighbors that might produce generative dialogue and mutual learning[19] are sacrificed for a more pragmatic approach that helps to ensure the bottom line.

---

19. Branson and Warnes, *Starting Missional Churches*.

Charismatic Leadership and Missional Change

Interestingly, Pastor Steve seems to realize that not all of these events accomplish his goal. He admits, for example, that "Church Without Walls is not great evangelistically. But it is effective for communicating that we'll get out of the box for our neighborhood. It may be good for pre-evangelism. We collected cards and gave out fifty-five boxes of food. We can follow-up with each of them." This quote reveals something in Pastor Steve that has been shifting: a realization that more than just events are needed to see meaningful transformation occur in the church's neighborhood—meaningful, ongoing relationships are needed as well.

While it is unlikely that Pastor Steve and The Lighthouse will ever do away with large neighborhood events completely, Pastor Steve seems to realize that more process oriented programs and relationships are needed to see the kind of sustainable change he is hoping for in the community. He revealed this realization further in another discussion, acknowledging that while "the church does events way more effectively than ongoing relational ministry with people in the community, [he is] hopeful that the community center and our small groups will change that." This is why he has fully supported the pursuit of ongoing partnerships with the Port City municipal office and other local individuals and entities to provide meaningful services for her neighbors. It is also why he encouraged the leadership council to approve a strategic partnership with Mark Smalls to begin MECA—the charter school that rents and occupies the building on the campus that housed The Lighthouse's Christian school for several decades.

Perhaps no other initiative symbolizes The Lighthouse's emerging commitment to engage its neighborhood as its place through partnerships better than The Lighthouse's relationship with MECA. Launched in the Fall of 2008 as a charter school focusing on entrepreneurship through microenterprise for inner-city middle school children, MECA is the culmination of a dream for Mark Smalls. A former professional football player, current pastor, and entrepreneur, Mark forged a partnership with The Lighthouse through a process facilitated through a current Lighthouse member. Dean, a lay leader at The Lighthouse who had known Mark for several years through some initiatives they had worked on together with inner-city youth, knew Mark had been looking for a location for his charter school since 2006. He also knew that The Lighthouse now had a vacant school building since closing its elementary school down in 2006. Sensing an opportunity for both parties, he arranged an introduction between Mark, Pastors Steve and Peter, and Cathy Downs, a member of the leadership council, near the end of 2007.

Leadership Resources Driving Change at The Lighthouse

According to Dean, that meeting and a subsequent site visit for Mark "was the genesis for a potential collaboration between Mark and The Lighthouse. They began to dream to open collaboration and information sharing... and Mark and Steve both saw the possibilities for mentoring and a volunteer program at MECA with The Lighthouse." From that point on, things began moving fairly rapidly. According to Cathy, Pastor Steve used his influence with the leadership council to get the partnership proposal between the school and the church approved. The charter was then approved by the state in the summer of 2008, and the school began that fall.

To ensure that collaboration would occur between the two groups, Pastor Steve and Mark came to an agreement on several vital points. According to Pastor Steve, they agreed to a lease that was 40 percent under market value to cement the fact that this was a partnership, not a rental. They also agreed that there would be three Lighthouse members on the board of the school, a Lighthouse member on the staff, and that Mark would preach occasionally in the church. Since then, there have been signs of a burgeoning partnership. Recalling some of the things that had occurred since the school opened in the fall of 2008, Pastor Steve recounted:

> Some of the kids from MECA come to Fusion, our youth ministry during the week, and some of our church kids attend the school. This year, we raised $1,200 one Sunday, to send the 8th graders to Magic Mountain for a graduation party the following week, and we held another fundraiser in May. We also ran a joint basketball league this year, with three to four teams from MECA and three to four teams from the community through Paul. Our people refereed and volunteered to run the tournament. We also did a joint beautification project in a nearby neighborhood. I believe this is just the tip of the iceberg!

According to several respondents, plans are also underway to launch an afterschool program that will offer tutoring, computer courses, leadership training, ongoing sports leagues and classes in the creative arts, games, and other activities. While there is still a long way to go, it seems that the surface is just being scratched at the potential that is available for future ministry.

As The Lighthouse's mission theology has continued to manifest into a commitment to its place over the last few years, it has also become more holistic. That is, it has begun to focus not just on proclamation of the Gospel as central to mission but also on meeting the socio-emotional, relational, and

Charismatic Leadership and Missional Change

physical needs of the whole person; addressing injustice and societal ills; and engaging in creation care. This holistic view of mission has begun to shape how The Lighthouse tangibly engages its community on mission, which I have discussed throughout the last two chapters. Some of the programs that highlight this shift are those involving the community center: things like computer training and other educational initiatives for at-risk youth. Others include The Lighthouse's partnerships and community-based initiatives like MECA, neighborhood beautification, and community fairs, and its commitment to health and creation care a the community garden.

Lynette's words illustrate the holistic aspects of the Lighthouse's emerging mission theology well.

> God's desire is to have a deep relationship with humanity and for that relationship to be reciprocated.... The role of believers is to invite others into that relationship based on God's great love for people and the world, and who He is. The Church's role in God's mission is to be God's presence in the world. Christ incarnate in the world is the role of the church. That includes justice, compassion, love, peace, and hope. Ultimately the church should reflect these things even though not perfect. Justice and evangelism need to go hand in hand. Christ's love is expressed the most effectively when the Church is involved in service, justice, and love in the world. Actions speak louder than words. Is evangelism important? Absolutely. But they need to work together so that people know the motivation behind the justice. The message is very important, but it is expressed best through these things. But some people forget the message when so focused on justice. They need to work together.

Evidenced in the theologizing above is the reality that The Lighthouse has slowly begun to discover and embody an increasingly holistic understanding of mission that harkens back to its roots in the beginning of the Free Methodist movement. During the time that BT Roberts founded the fledgling denomination in 1860, it was in large part because of the mainline Methodist church's refusal to take up the cause of slaves by participating in the abolition movement; its refusal to take up the cause of the poor by eliminating pew taxes; and its refusal to take up the cause of women by giving them the right to pursue ministry according to their giftedness. The early Free Methodists had a strong commitment to issues of social justice, to education, to extending mercy and fair treatment to the poor, and of course, to the proclamation of the Gospel.[20] Evangelism and justice were both a crucial

20. Marston, *Living Witness*.

part of the Gospel and God's mission. One thing we notice in Lynette's words is a strong commitment to a holistic sense of mission that values evangelism and justice equally. For Lynette, they are inseparable. One without the other would somehow distort the love of God in the world.

Would the other respondents answer with this same holistic understanding of God's mission to the world? While there is variance in degree, as well as the ability to theologically articulate this view, the answer to this question is yes. Eleven of thirteen interview respondents expressed a value for God's love to be extended in tangible ways by the church as it carries out God's mission in its community. Pastor Ella, for example, asserted that "extending God's mercy by distributing food and meeting the needs of people is an essential part of the church carrying out God's mission," and that her "desire to see urban kids have access to healthy food was a motivating factor for beginning the community garden." In fact, aside from the community center and the partnership with MECA, perhaps no ongoing initiative reveals The Lighthouse's commitment to its surrounding community as its place than the community garden Pastor Ella began on the church's campus in March 2010.

The excitement in Pastor Ella's face is obvious as I talk with her. In fact, the more she talks, the more obvious it becomes that this is someone who has discovered something that they are really passionate about.

> I strongly believe that a theology of beauty is a central part of God's mission. Basically, what I am doing is co-creating with God in this project. I'm taking the position, "Let's co-create with God together." It's amazing. It's like maybe I was created to do this, to influence leaders through a garden!

Since March of 2010, Pastor Ella has been using this garden to catalyze people in the church to a new way of experiencing life. She has also been using it to introduce people in the community not just to healthy food, but also to the Creator God who wants to co-create with them.

The community garden is in many ways symbolic of the journey that The Lighthouse is on toward a new missional identity—it was unexpected and is breaking some paradigms held by those in The Lighthouse about what it means for a church to be on mission in a diverse urban area. It has drawn some unexpected interest from urbanites in the congregation, for example, who are re-connecting with the Creator God in new ways as they serve in the garden and see the fruits of their labors—fresh vegetables they are not used to getting in their inner-city grocery stores. Pastor Ella beams, for example, when she talks about two men—one of them a Christian hip-hop artist in the congregation—who have both been volunteering regularly in the garden with excitement. It represents a more holistic sense of mission that the church is moving toward—seeing that God's mission is about redeeming all of creation, not just people. She smiles as she shares about her hopes for starting a contemplative garden on one of the more violent streets near the church so that peaceful community can be created in the midst of a violent neighborhood as God works to redeem it. It also represents holistic mission through God's mercy as fresh vegetables are harvested weekly to replenish the food pantry, as people from the community are invited to come harvest for their personal use throughout the week, and as fresh vegetables are distributed to congregants in need every Sunday at church.

The community garden is also serving as a catalyst for new missional partnerships in ways that are quite surprising. The garden was forged in partnership with friends of Pastors Ella and Steve who brought a mission team down from Seattle to help build the 11 x 120 foot garden in less than a week in what was formerly a weed bed in MECA's playground. Curriculum is currently being developed so that MECA can incorporate it into its micro-enterprise curriculum. Due to a new city by-law, it has created an opportunity to plant a larger quarter-acre garden in Reyes Park, a dangerous and somewhat barren city-owned and operated park a mile up the street where the church holds its Bible Fiesta Fun and Church Without Walls events every year. Just as important, the garden has provided a venue for forming relationships and listening to neighbors as church participants work and attend to God's initiatives in their midst. Who would have thought that a little green could produce so much fruit?

Another question remains in light of the larger discussion here, however. How do some of the other respondents articulate a commitment to holistic mission? Pastor Peter noted that the church's mission should comprise both evangelism and a social justice component to it, citing examples like partnering with non-profits and agencies to effect positive change in schools, poverty, and other forms of injustice. Similarly, Betty emphasized that "God's mission is to communicate his love to people in a holistic sense, [both] in and beyond the community," while Dean quoted one of his favorite scriptures to highlight his belief: "Religion that God our Father accepts as pure and faultless is this: to look after orphans and widows in their distress and to keep oneself from being polluted by the world" (Jas 1:27).

Many in the congregation seem to share this emphasis on holistic mission as well. Of the survey respondents, 51.8 percent said that the main priority of the church should be to provide compassionate ministries that will meet the needs of people in the church's community, and 89.5 percent either agree or strongly agree with the statement, "Our single biggest priority is to learn how to love and serve our diverse neighbors more effectively."

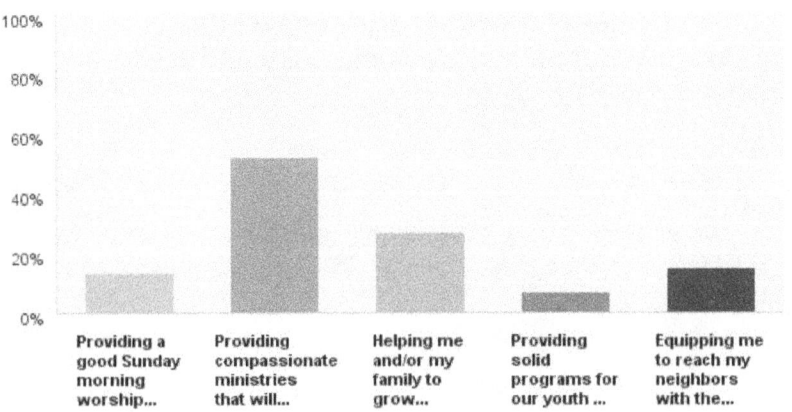

Q11 **What do you believe the main priority of our church should be?**

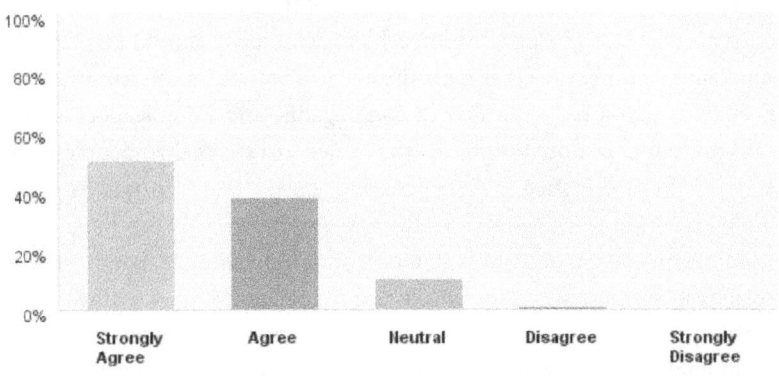

Q16 **One of the leaders in the church has said, "Our single biggest priority is to learn how to love and serve our diverse neighbors more effectively."**

Similarly, 86 percent agree or strongly agree that, "Our church should form partnerships with individuals, local agencies, and other churches to truly impact those living in our immediate community and area." These numbers are quite strong, and they reveal how deeply many within the congregation hold this understanding of mission.

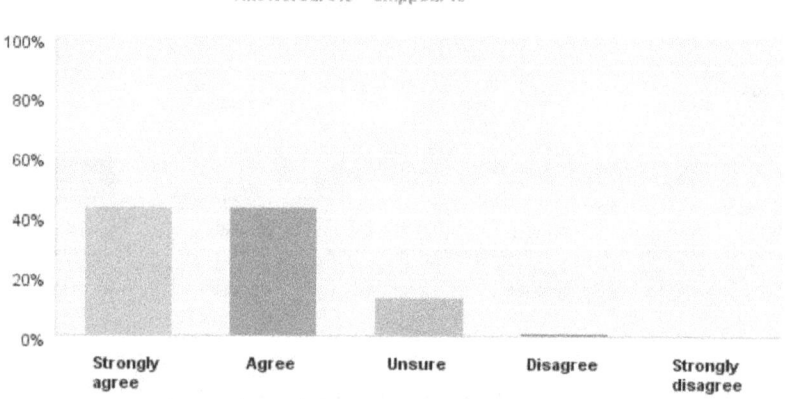

In spite of these strong numbers and the positions of the respondents articulated above, there is a level of variation in the degree to which some share in this holistic view of mission. Through my interactions with many congregants—possibly represented by some of the 48.2 percent of survey respondents who don't believe the church's main priority should be providing compassionate ministries that meet the needs of people in the community—it is obvious that a large number of congregants, and some leaders as well, would place much more emphasis on the need to evangelize people rather than work toward justice and compassion. Pastor Steve, in fact, is one of those who would seem to favor a stronger emphasis on evangelism. While he told me on several occasions that acts of mercy and love like those Jesus describes in his parable of the sheep and the goats (Matt 25:31–46) are an essential part of the church's mission, in the interview I referenced earlier in this chapter, his preference for evangelism is clear.

Leadership Resources Driving Change at The Lighthouse

Ultimately, what this illustrates is the nature of The Lighthouse's journey. The holistic aspect of the missional theology of place that is currently emerging within the church is a recent development that continues to mature among both the staff and congregants. Some pastors and leaders are further along the spectrum toward holistic mission than others, as are many in the congregation. As the church continues its journey toward becoming a community-based and community-focused church, and as its demographics continue to shift more and more toward reflecting its ethnically diverse neighborhood, its theology will likely continue to shift toward a more holistic understanding of mission as well.

The progress that The Lighthouse has seen in its mission theology will likely continue to face some significant obstacles as it continues its journey toward a mission-actional praxis, however. I have demonstrated throughout this discussion the struggle that Pastor Steve has been going through as the schema informing his philosophy of ministry has been challenged during the process. He acknowledges the challenges associated with centering mission activities in the neighborhood on relationships and process over events, for example, when he admits the tension he feels financially when considering attractional versus missional or relational. "I love the emphasis on missional and have heartily embraced that, but I feel the tension when we start going that way. . . . The tension here is from my desire to see numerical growth, more results quicker, especially conversions." His comments here reveal the competing commitments that are hindering him from fully embracing the new practices that he senses are important for The Lighthouse to continue on its journey toward missional. On the one hand, he has a growing desire to see God transform the church's neighborhood. This desire is tempered, however, by his concern for solidifying the church's viability moving forward. Similarly, his slowly increasing commitment toward increasing ongoing ministries in the community is tempered by his unwillingness to completely give up the type of ministries that fit into his pre-existing ministry schema.

The challenge for Pastor Steve and The Lighthouse is that over time, a commitment to maintaining both can be problematic. Large events consume large amounts of time and energy, from staff and volunteers alike, and put a strain on limited church budgets. This drain on resources can impact a church's ability to adequately fund and support ongoing ministries, and it can ultimately steal the resources necessary to support ongoing initiatives.[21]

21. Rainer and Geiger, *Simple Church*.

Charismatic Leadership and Missional Change

Likewise, congregational involvement in ongoing ministries can over time have the same detrimental effect on events when balance between the two lacks. What this highlights is that at some point in the near future, it may be necessary for Pastor Steve and the staff to make a choice. They may either need to commit fully to a path towards missional as understood by those in one of the other branches of the missional tree, or continue trying to both. As their ministry schema continues to be challenged, this change can become easier to embrace if they participate in reflective practices together so that they can engage in praxis. The problem is that, right now, Pastor Steve does not provide the construction sites necessary for this to happen on a staff or corporate level. This will come into focus as I explore how Pastor Steve and the ministry staff have been attempting to construct a missional theology of place among the congregation.

Constructing Theology through Vision Casting, Service, and Hiring

Understanding the holistic nature of the commitment to place that The Lighthouse is attempting to live out in North Port City, how have Pastor Steve and the rest of the leadership team gone about constructing this missional theology of place within the congregation? They have utilized three primary means—continual vision casting, service opportunities, and hiring staff members that better reflect the neighborhood ethnically.

As I discussed briefly in the introduction, a great deal of leadership literature lifts up the value of casting vision to inspire and drive change in congregations.[22] Likewise, a great deal of the literature from practitioners and scholars in the multiethnic church movement does as well.[23] As someone who fits the descriptors assigned to charismatic leaders discussed earlier in this chapter, vision casting is one of Pastor Steve's strengths. This was readily acknowledged by several Ministry Staff Leaders (MSL's) and lay leaders that I interviewed. Vision—and some of its derivatives—was in fact the most popular word used to describe Steve when I asked my interview subjects to describe his leadership style. This can obviously be a great strength or a hindrance for leaders, as I discussed in my literature review in chapter 1. In

---

22. See Malphurs, *Vision for Ministry*; Southerland, *Transitioning*; Herrington, Bonem, and Furr, *Leading Congregational Change*.

23. See Kujawa-Holbrook, *House of Prayer*; Ortiz, *One New People*; Foster, *Embracing Diversity*.

the case of Pastor Steve, it appears to have been a great asset as he has tried to construct a missional theology of place at The Lighthouse.

During the course of my research, I had the opportunity to attend a leadership council meeting, four staff meetings, and several services. As a member of the church for four years and as a former employee for one, I had the chance to participate in more than 150 services and sit in on dozens of staff meetings. During these times, I was able to see, and often experience firsthand, Pastor Steve's ability to cast vision effectively and passionately. As I described in chapter 2, the church was able to raise $120,000 in one month to pay for renovations to the community center, primarily due to Pastor Steve's ability to cast vision from the pulpit during Sunday services. Similarly, there were several times in staff meetings when he was able to sway the room in favor of his vision for a particular initiative or, conversely, to convince those in the room that a competing vision was not the way to go. Betty illustrates his ability with these words: "If Steve doesn't buy in, it won't happen."

As the church began and, ultimately, continued its transition into mission-actional ministry, it was readily apparent to all what Pastor Steve wanted and where he sensed the church needing to go. In meetings, he regularly lifted up the value of engaging the surrounding community on mission and began to integrate missional living into his messages on Sunday mornings regularly. His unique gifts and personality traits allowed him to cast this vision regularly in ways that did not guilt people but rather inspired them to reach for more in their lives. One such example was the implementation of Heroes of the Faith, a weekly video series that highlighted an individual in the Sunday service that fellow members had nominated and voted for as someone who exemplified missional living. Using means such as this, Pastor Steve and the leadership team were able to cast vision by including the congregation in the process by holding up positive examples of change rather than berating people with what they weren't doing or "guilting" them into more intentional living.

In my interviews, several leaders affirmed these characteristics in Pastor Steve. Sandra, for example, said that, "Steve is someone with vision and gets the team to buy in. His greatest strength is positivity. He believes we can do it!" Similarly, Betty asserts that, "Steve is a charismatic leader who carries vision. If he has it, people follow it. . . . He is a dynamic leader who wants the church connected to the community and he communicates that as best as he can. His greatest strength is that he is a visionary, and he communicates that vision really well from the pulpit." Because of this, he was often able to push people out of their comfort zones while providing the encouragement necessary to get staff and congregants alike to believe they could do it.

This view is not just held by key leaders, however. It also appears to be shared by the majority of those in the congregation. While none of the questions in my survey asked congregants to speak directly into Steve's ability to cast vision and communicate, their responses when asked to share their current views about the direction of the church are revealing. A staggering 94.9 percent of congregants said that they are either excited about or feel positive about the current direction of the church. This figure speaks implicitly toward their feelings about the vision Pastor Steve is casting for the future of the church, and the results seem to be paying off. As I previously noted, 51.8 percent of those surveyed feel that the main priority of the church should be to provide compassionate ministries that meet the needs of those in the church's community, and 88.5 percent believe that the single biggest priority of the church should be to learn how to love and serve the church's diverse neighbors. Obviously, many in the congregation seem to be accepting the message they perceive Pastor Steve to be delivering to them.

Pastor Steve and the staff have not just relied on vision casting to embed the value of place at The Lighthouse, however. They have also attempted to reinforce new mission-actional values and practices by connecting congregants to service opportunities in the community. One example of this is Serve the City, an annual one-day event that mobilizes several churches throughout the city to serve people and groups in the community through tangible acts of service. Several interview respondents, including Pastor Steve, acknowledged that this service project doesn't really have that much sustainable impact on the community, but that its main value is to expose members of the church to some of the greater needs in the community. It also gives them a chance to experience what it is like to get out outside the walls of the church and serve others. Other annual events like Bible Fiesta Fun, Church Without Walls, and occasional community projects and beautification day's function in similar ways.

One of the primary ways that they maximize these events is by connecting as many people as possible in the congregation into these opportunities according to their giftedness and interests. Enter Charlene Donner and the Volunteer Service Corps (VSC). The VSC—a database of people willing to serve with their availability, their skills and passions, and experiences—is Charlene's brainchild. It was born out of some of her own difficult ministry experiences, as well as the experiences of others who had impacted her. In her own words, she "created the VSC to catalyze people into service for the Kingdom in the church and in the community, according to their passions and giftedness" because she was tired of seeing people misused and burned out.

Charlene—an African American professional woman nearing retirement who has been at The Lighthouse with her husband for over fifteen years—has been serving in the church in some capacity for over twelve of them. She has quite often served in multiple roles at once, including stints serving on the leadership council, as a teacher for LIFE Classes, and in several other ministries. Pastor Steve and other ministry staff weren't shy about approaching Charlene to serve in other ways as well, as they viewed her as a high capacity volunteer. Not surprisingly, she decided to step down from her ministry responsibilities in 2009, as she felt like she was burning out from ministry. As she shared the situation with me, she simply said, "I was tired. I needed some time to rest, discern my passion and the skills I had to offer in ministry, and how to invest myself in my next phase of life after retirement. I spent the first part of 2009 simply thinking and praying about these things."

Something interesting happened next though. One of the pastors kept approaching her to coordinate Serve the City in spite of her consistent refusals. In spite of her fatigue, she finally relented and agreed to do it. Little did she know that this would change the course of her ministry future as a volunteer in the church.

> It was a huge task. Very challenging and time consuming. By the time it was over I was exhausted, but I was on a high. I loved it! I was energized in spite of the hard work as I realized that my professional skills applied so well. I realized that this was my niche, my sweet spot. I started asking myself, "How can I do this?" I just thought it was so cool helping others identify their skills and passions and connecting them to a need. Then I started wondering how we could bridge the gap between the church and the community from what I saw in Serve the City and sent an email to Pastor Steve.

After an iterative process developing a plan with feedback from Pastor Steve and then the executive team, Charlene launched VSC at the end of 2009 with a $4,000 budget. Not wanting to repeat the mistakes of the

Charismatic Leadership and Missional Change

past, however, she recruited a team of seven gifted leaders who shared her passion for mobilizing God's people into tangible action. Since the launch, she and her team have guided the VSC to place hundreds of volunteers into service opportunities, both inside and outside of the church. While most are project-based, some are ongoing, and she excitedly shared how the VSC had placed many people—lots of whom were never involved in ministry—into opportunities.

> We organized forty to fifty volunteers for the grand opening of the community center in June. We were able to plug over 150 people into Serve the City projects in May. We have been able to connect a bunch of people into CWOW, IC Kids, Sharing Meals, the CUE Conference[24] in the spring, and the community garden to name just a few. We now have 175 people and about a dozen service opportunities in the database, and oversee Serve the City every year.

The excitement flowing through Charlene as she shared story after story was infectious, and it was clear that she had found her niche in the church's journey toward increased mission engagement with the community at large. She is a connector and mobilizer, helping Pastor Steve implement his vision of turning The Lighthouse into a church of, with, and for the community.

As the focus on the immediate community surrounding the church continued, intentional hires at the ministry staff level also contributed toward and reinforced the commitment to place in The Lighthouse's mission focus. Pastors Steve and Ella both mentioned that they brought Paul and Tina Maeva, a Samoan couple that lives in the community, on to the pastoral staff to increase the church's influence in their community. As they established themselves as leaders in the church, Pastor Steve gave them more freedom and support to lead the church into community-based ministry. According to Pastor Steve,

> God started saying to me, "What are you doing in your own neighborhood?" Ella and I were being prompted through prayer for the church and through Ella's DMin. We began empowering Paul and Tina more and raising awareness among our church for community needs.

---

24. Continental Urban Exchange is a Free Methodist urban ministry leaders fellowship.

Similarly, Pastor Ella noted that, "Paul and Tina took it to the streets in their truck to Reyes, Hale, and Southpointe.[25] Paul and Tina have been a huge influence to the community, through IC Kidz, sports outreaches here and in the parks, and now through the community center."

Pastors Steve and Ella also both mentioned the importance of bringing Xavier, a Spanish-speaking pastor, on to the staff. According to Pastor Steve, "We began raising awareness among our church for community needs... so we brought on Xavier because of our desire to reach the Hispanic community. They represent the largest demographic in our one-mile radius, but they are probably the most under-represented in the congregation." Soon after, Xavier launched *Norte*, a bi-lingual service in Spanish and English targeting first and second generation Hispanics in the neighborhood in 2009.

The new staff hires weren't done, however. Lynette shared how hiring a Nigerian male, a Panamanian woman, and a bi-racial woman (African American/Caucasian) over the previous few years had helped the ministry staff to better reflect the community. While the staff is still predominantly white, Lynette shared that there is definite progress being made. As the staff has become more reflective of the surrounding community, they have helped to reinforce place as the locus of The Lighthouse's mission efforts among the congregation because they better understand the needs of those in the community and the opportunities that are present.

Assessing the Commitment to a Missional Theology of Place at The Lighthouse

According to the raw data generated by my survey, it would appear that pastoral leadership at The Lighthouse has been fairly successful at constructing a missional theology of place among congregants—at least intellectually. As I mentioned earlier in this chapter, when asked whether they agreed with the statement, "Our single biggest priority is to learn how to love and serve our diverse neighbors more effectively," 88.5 percent of the respondents indicated that they agreed or strongly agreed. Likewise, in two related questions, 65.5 percent of respondents said they believe that the community surrounding the church should be the primary focus of the church's mission activities, and 86 percent believe that the church should form strategic partnerships to positively impact those living in the church's community. Further, when asked what they felt the main priority of the

---

25. Hale and Southpointe are low-income apartments in North Port City within one or two miles of the church.

church should be, 66.8 percent of respondents indicated that it should be to either provide compassionate ministries to meet the needs of those in the community or to equip church members to share the gospel with their neighbors.

These findings are encouraging and indicate that many in the congregation seem to have a value for the church to embody a missional theology of place in their community. But what does the data reveal about the congregation's lived practices? In short, it reveals that the practices of many congregants do not yet match their theology. In other words, a gap exists between their espoused and lived values—an espoused value for missional life and the current lived expressions that exists in the congregation. There are several reasons for this, including an absence of construction sites for corporate reflection that would allow both staff and leaders to engage in praxis. I will explore this and other contributing factors in-depth in chapters 4 and 5.

SUMMARY

In this chapter, I have discussed two of the primary resources utilized by pastoral leadership to drive the change process toward mission-actional ministry at The Lighthouse—the charismatic leadership approach, utilized by Pastor Steve to influence his followers, and the missional theology of place that he and the pastoral staff have been constructing within the congregation. In doing so, I have spoken to the issue of why Pastor Steve and the pastoral team lead change the way they do at the Lighthouse. The leadership and ministry schemas that shape Pastor Steve and the pastoral team's leadership philosophy and missional imagination allow him to play to his strengths—utilizing his charismatic influence to inspire and drive change in the congregation. This allows him to lead in a way that is comfortable for him—in top-down ways that allow him to cast vision and inspire his followers.

As I have highlighted how Pastor Steve's charismatic approach toward leadership has facilitated the church forward on its journey toward mission-actional, I have also touched on some of the challenges created by his leadership style. I alluded to the fact that Pastor Steve and other ministry leaders at The Lighthouse need to learn new values and engage in new practices as they lead if they wish to avoid some of the pitfalls of charismatic leadership, especially if they wish to close the perceived gap between lived and preferred values pertaining to embodying a missional theology of place in the community. In the next chapter, I will analyze the nature of the adaptive challenges facing the pastoral staff as they continue to lead The Lighthouse on its journey. In doing so, I will begin to build a case that the pastors and ministry leaders at The Lighthouse need to shift their approach if they desire to sustain their transformation into a mission-actional church or attain their stated goal of becoming missional.

4

Adaptive Challenges at The Lighthouse

It should be apparent by now that the Lighthouse has made some significant progress on its journey toward mission-actional. The resources Pastor Steve has used to drive change have begun to re-define the schemas that are shaping The Lighthouse's mission praxis. Consequently, Pastor Steve and the pastoral staff have started to address the adaptive challenge of placeless-ness that is shaping their context and their congregational life. What I will demonstrate in this chapter, however, is that the resources Pastor Steve has been using have contributed toward three other adaptive challenges that the church will need to address. The first is a gap between a lived and preferred value for mission in the congregation. The second is the congregation's over-dependence on the charismatic leader. The third is the Euro-centric leadership schema that is shaping leadership selection and development by the staff. All three of these challenges are hindering the ethnically diverse congregation's participation in the process of missional change at the Lighthouse and fit into Heifetz, Grashow and Linsky's first adaptive archetype—"a gap between espoused values and behaviors."

A GAP BETWEEN A LIVED AND PREFERRED VALUE FOR MISSIONAL

As I discussed in chapter 3, many congregants at The Lighthouse seem to hold a preferred value for a missional theology of place. Yet, I also suggested that this preferred value has not necessarily translated into lived reality in a majority of congregants' lives. When asked how often they spend meaningful time with their neighbors or engage with their local community, for example, only 27.9 percent of respondents indicated that they do so at least two to three times per month, and fewer than 50 percent do so on at least a monthly basis. Further, over 52 percent of respondents indicated that they only "occasionally" (two to three times per year or less), or "rarely" (once per year or less) spend meaningful time with their neighbors or engaging with their local community.

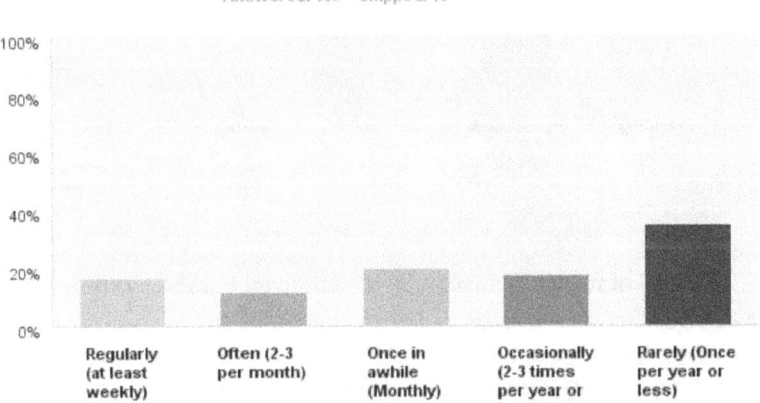

Similarly, while approximately half of the respondents indicated that they are more involved with their neighbors and local community than they were two to three years ago, the other half indicated that they are either involved at the same level or actually less involved. Thus, while this seemingly conflicting data indicates reason for optimism in the progress that has been made with half of the congregation, it is also somewhat disconcerting that such a high percentage (over 25 percent) of the congregation has actually regressed in their commitment to forming meaningful relationships with their neighbors and getting involved with their community.

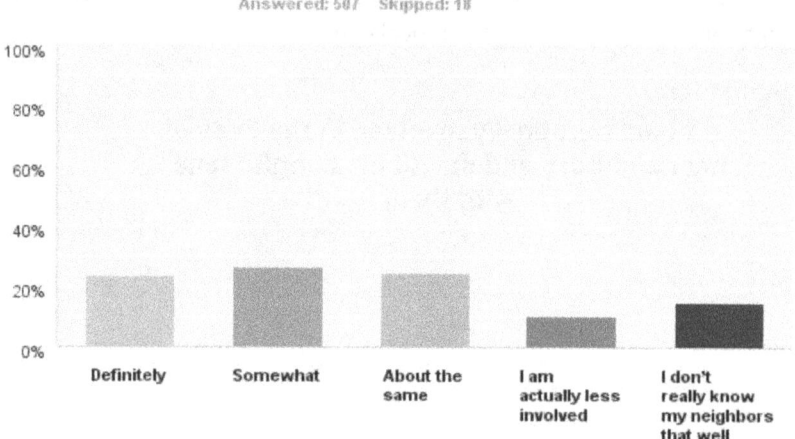

The level of relational involvement with neighbors is not the only way that this gap between a lived and preferred value for mission-actional is demonstrated by congregants at The Lighthouse, however. It is also revealed in the level of church involvement—specifically through service. According to the survey data, 3.8 percent of respondents are leading a ministry team and only 18.7 percent are currently serving on a team of any kind.[1] Further, only a small percentage of these people seem to actually be involved in outreach ministries outside the walls of the church. The overwhelming majority of those who are involved in some sort of ministry instead appear to serve in church-centered ministries on Sunday mornings and Wednesday evenings during services, including children and youth ministries, worship teams, and other Sunday morning service teams. Accounting for some redundancy between those leading and serving on a team, this means that 80 percent or more of congregants are not involved in any type of ministry inside or outside of the church, choosing instead to participate primarily in weekend worship services and possibly in a small group. The majority of those who are involved in a ministry tend to focus their service on those already inside the walls of the church.

1. See Figure 7 in chapter 1.

What this reveals is that the overwhelming majority of congregants at The Lighthouse appear to be religious consumers, attending church primarily for what they receive on Sundays rather than giving of themselves in service to others. Those who are serving primarily serve those within the church. The work of compassion and outreach appears best left to the professionals whom they pay to develop these types of ministries. I will discuss this more in the following section when I discuss the clergy-centered ministry schema that is informing the church's mission praxis.

When considered with the previous discussion regarding the level of neighbor involvement, it seems clear, then, that while leadership has indeed made progress toward embedding a theology of place among congregants, there is a gap between what a significant number of congregants believe and what they do to live this theology out. The question that needs to be answered, then, is why does this gap between belief and practice at The Lighthouse exist? The answer to this question, I believe, lies in the second adaptive challenge revealed in the data—over-dependence on the charismatic leader.

OVER-DEPENDENCE ON THE CHARISMATIC LEADER

According to the data, the gap between a lived and preferred value for mission-actional among congregants at The Lighthouse may be explained by the leadership schema that is shaping the mission praxis of the church. The top-down, clergy-centered understanding of leadership appears to be contributing toward an over-dependence on the pastoral staff for ministry, especially relating to mission initiatives, creativity, and innovation in the community. Further, this clergy-centered understanding of ministry seems to be held and lived out by congregants and pastoral leadership alike, albeit in different ways.

Commitment to Clergy-Centered Mission Praxis

According to the survey data, 54 percent of the survey respondents said that it is the responsibility of the pastoral staff and other church leaders to reach people in the community, while only 31.6 percent viewed it as their own responsibility.

Charismatic Leadership and Missional Change

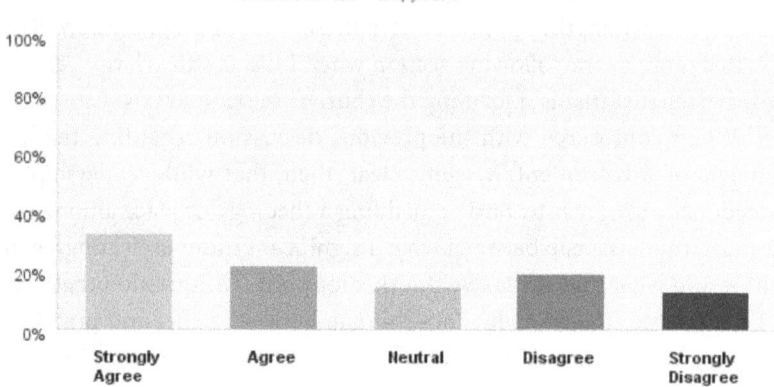

While this clergy-centered view of ministry held by more than half of the congregation should not be entirely surprising considering the level of congregational involvement discussed previously, it is revealing when considered alongside congregant's expressed views regarding the mission focus of the church. As I noted previously, 66 percent of respondents said that the church should form partnerships to impact the lives of people in the immediate community,[2] and 88.5 percent agreed or strongly agreed that the single biggest priority of the church should be learning how to love and serve the diverse neighbors of the church.[3] Further, 66.5 percent said that the immediate area surrounding the church should be the primary focus of the church's mission activity.

---

2. See Figure 10 in chapter 3.
3. See Figure 9 in chapter 3.

Adaptive Challenges at The Lighthouse

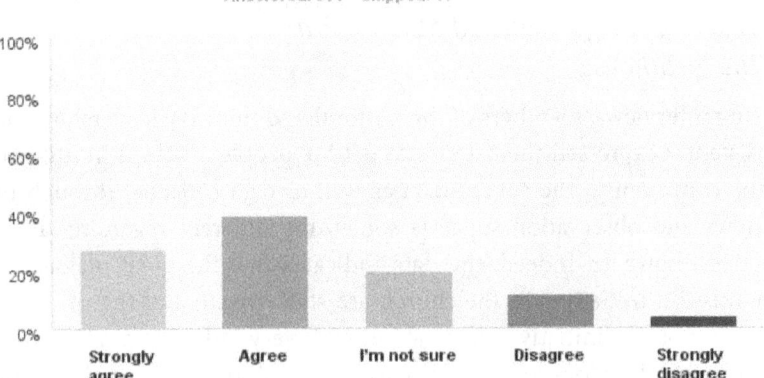

This indicates that the majority of congregants hold to an espoused value for local mission and see the importance of the church reaching the immediate community with the gospel. Yet, when considered with the percentage of respondents putting the responsibility for outreach on the pastoral staff and other church leaders as well as the percentage of congregants actually involved in some aspect of local mission, it also reveals that the majority of congregants view this task as the responsibility of someone else—church leadership.

Congregants' views on this issue at The Lighthouse should not be surprising considering how consumerism shapes the American cultural context.[4] Church attendees are shaped by the same consumerist values as their neighbors and bring those same values into their religious practice. We see this evidenced in many areas of congregational life, such as voluntary segregation along ethnic lines and through "church shopping."[5] It also appears to reinforce this cycle of dependency on church leadership and the clergy-centered ministry schema that is informing it, as it is more comfortable for congregants to passively sit and consume religious goods and services as the paid professionals do the work of ministry. Pastoral leadership at The Lighthouse is facing a strong challenge as they try to address this particular

4. Barber, *Consumed*.
5. Metzger, *Consuming Jesus*.

adaptive challenge, then, as an embedded cultural value seems to be reinforcing it. This is not the only challenge, however, as the data reveals that the practices of the pastoral staff may also be reinforcing this schema.

Reinforcing Clergy-Centered Mission Praxis at The Lighthouse

During interviews, members of the pastoral and ministry leadership team consistently expressed their desire to get lay-people involved in ministry in the community. The survey data as well as data collected through interviews and observation suggests something different regarding actual practices, however. Indeed, the data indicates that the great majority of new mission initiatives in the church are staff driven, and that more often than not, the initiatives came about with very little, if any, input from congregants. This top-down approach to leadership, which I have already discussed at length, reinforces the clergy-centered leadership schema at The Lighthouse and ultimately hinders missional innovation and creativity within the congregation.

Alan Roxburgh and Fred Romanuk suggest that missional innovation occurs in congregations as leaders cultivate dialogue and listening across the system. Conversely, when leaders rely on their own discernment and ability to interpret the situation, they thwart creativity and innovation among their followers because they create dependency on their plans and leadership.[6] This appears to be the case at The Lighthouse. For example, when asked whether they had ever been approached by leadership for insights into their neighbors or how they sensed God at work in their community, over 46 percent of respondents answered never. While this might seem like a low number considering the size of the congregation, the structure of the question and my interview data suggests that this number may actually be quite high. For example, two survey respondents who answered "several times" in response to the question wrote extraneous comments on their survey documents beside their answers. Sharing the sentiment of the other respondent, one stated, "But never by the pastors." The inference here is that while lay leaders in the church had approached these individuals several times, they had never been approached by a member of the pastoral staff. Assuming that these two respondents were not alone in their broad interpretation of the term "leader" utilized in the question (indicating a design flaw in my

---

6. Roxburgh and Romanuk, *Missional Leader*, 26–35.

question), the number of those who have never been approached by pastoral leadership is likely quite a bit higher than the data indicated.

This interpretation is supported more directly through my interview data, as most of the staff indicated that they rarely, if ever, consulted lay people when beginning new mission initiatives in their ministry areas. Instead, they thought about the idea themselves; got the idea from a book, a conference, or during their formal education; talked with other pastors on the staff about the idea; or, in a few cases, discussed it with a select group of lay leaders on their leadership teams. On those occasions when lay leaders were consulted, it was often during the design and implementation phases later in the process or for feedback rather than for ideas. As I discussed earlier, Pastor Steve, for example, indicated that his preferred leadership style is to propose decisions and/or solutions, gather some feedback, and then make a decision. He usually assesses the situation in advance and often comes to a meeting with his mind made up regarding his preferred course of action. While he indicated that he is trying to shift to a more team-based approach that makes joint decisions with the team as equals, he acknowledged that this has been a difficult transition for him.

This mode of decision-making and discernment also seems to be characteristic of others in the staff as well. Through the interviews and observations during my first phase of research, I was unable to discern any environments created by the staff where missional ideas held by congregants could be uncovered and nurtured. Unless a pastoral leader took the time to solicit ideas from individuals one at a time—which my research did not uncover—then those ideas appear to remain latent in the congregation. There are also examples, however, where direct actions of staff served to reinforce this cycle of over-dependence on leadership by unwittingly suppressing missional innovation among the congregation as well. A pair of incidents three years apart with the community center illustrate this well.

The first incident occurred in 2007 with the taskforce that was formed to discern the mission focus of the center once it opened. The taskforce met weekly over the course of several months to gather and interpret data from The Lighthouse's immediate community to discern the greatest needs that The Lighthouse could meet through the community center. A few months into the process, a decision was made by Pastor Peter—who was leading the taskforce at that time—to bring in a computer-training ministry to use the space without input from the taskforce. Pastor Peter felt that the opportunity was too good to pass up and that, consequently, "we should go for it." The pushback he received from four of the six taskforce members present fell on deaf ears, and the decision was made. One respondent of the experience, Leroy, said, "We had more questions. Some people made the decision absent of what we thought. It can be dangerous to make decisions like that without the blessing of the group commissioned to make those recommendations. I remember thinking, "Why am I even here if these decisions can be made absent of feedback?" Betty shared those sentiments, musing that, "It makes you feel devalued when something like that happens. Why even put in your time?"

The second incident with the community center occurred early in 2010. Now that the center was finally set to open after the long work stoppage and renovations, a new taskforce was formed to once again discern the types of programs that the center would house. Against the wishes of the new taskforce, Pastor Peter pushed ahead a launch for the center even though the majority of the taskforce didn't think they were ready. One of the ministry staff leaders, for example, said, "We didn't even have any staffing or programs set up to follow-up with. It just felt like there was panic by Pastor Paul to get something going now. That was very frustrating. I said, hey, if we're gonna do it, why not wait and do it right? What are a couple more months?" Although the community center would ultimately begin some sustainable programs a few months later, this launch would ultimately turn out to be a false start, contributing toward more frustration on behalf of some members the taskforce and the larger church.

These two incidents in the history of what is arguably a positive symbol for The Lighthouse's journey toward a new vision of being a mission-actional church—the community center—serve to highlight some of the challenges resulting from the top-down, clergy-centered leadership schema that is shaping the mission praxis of the church. It demonstrates at least one tangible way how pastoral leadership has ultimately reinforced a cycle of dependency in the congregation, and how that cycle works to suppress missional innovation and creativity among lay-leaders. There is another factor that is shaping the mission-actional ethos in the church, however—a Euro-centric leadership schema that is affecting leadership selection and, consequently, contributing toward an ethnic hierarchy in the church.

A EURO-CENTRIC LEADERSHIP SCHEMA AND LEADERSHIP SELECTION

In the previous chapter I discussed the influence of an African American leader named Charlene who pioneered the Volunteer Service Corps at The Lighthouse. While it may seem counter-intuitive, Charlene's position and influence actually highlights another adaptive challenge at The Lighthouse—the way a Euro-centric leadership schema shaped by modern management frameworks is informing leadership selection in the church. As I mentioned previously, Charlene is considered to be a high capacity leader by Pastor Steve and several others on the ministry staff. Because of this, she has been consistently recruited for different, and sometimes multiple, leadership positions throughout her tenure at the church. The reason for this is that she appears to possess the leadership qualities valued by many in the senior ministry staff—she is a career business professional, educated and articulate, timely, responsible, self-motivated, a good communicator, and professional in appearance. Or, in the words of Pastor Peter, she is "sharp."

When seeking to identify cultural schemas, a helpful approach can be to identify key words and phrases that members of a particular cultural group use to describe a particular phenomenon, concept, idea, or value.[7] In the case of leadership selection and development, even positive key words used to describe members of a particular ethnic group that are not applied to members of other groups can be helpful, as their use can reveal not just values but also assumptions about particular groups of people. In this case, the use of the word sharp can help to uncover the nature of the Euro-centric leadership schema that is informing leadership selection processes at the church as well as underlying assumptions about particular groups of people. Pastor Peter, for example, a Caucasian senior leadership team member responsible for assimilation and leadership development in the church, used the word sharp several times during personal interactions with me over the last several years, as well as during our interview. In each case, he used the term to describe a key lay leader and, to the best of my knowledge, always in relationship to an African American lay leader he was recruiting for a leadership role. In each of these cases, the African American leader was a career professional, like Charlene, who displayed the personality and leadership traits that he valued for a particular leadership role.

Just as telling, however, are those to whom he does not direct the word—Caucasian leaders. When describing the qualities of Caucasian

---

7. Strauss and Quinn, *Cultural Meaning*.

leaders that he was either recruiting or had recently recruited, he stated that he looked for people who were "responsible, dependable, trustworthy, and who have good integrity." He did not, however, mention the word sharp in this list or during any of our other conversations. While this may seem potentially inconsequential, his use of the word sharp in relationship to leadership selection only with African Americans is revealing, especially when considered alongside the survey results relating to congregants' levels of involvement in the church along ethnic lines.

Perpetuating an Ethnic Hierarchy at The Lighthouse

A great deal of recent research highlights the negative impact that racial projects and schemas can have on congregational life in multiethnic churches and religious institutions, especially in relationship to church polity and leadership processes.[8] According to my survey data, the Lighthouse has not been exempt from these issues as it has continued on its journey toward mission-actional. The Euro-centric leadership schema that is informing leadership selection and development has helped to perpetuate an ethnic hierarchy within the church in spite of values and efforts to the contrary. A closer look at congregational involvement along ethnic lines supports this claim. For example, while 5.13 percent of Caucasian respondents indicated that they are currently leading a ministry team, just 1.4 percent of African Americans, 3.03 percent of Hispanics, and 4.17 percent of Asian/Pacific Islanders indicated the same.

---

8. See Edwards, *Elusive Dream*; Christerson, Edwards, and Emerson, *Against All Odds*.

TABLE 3

ETHNICITY AND LEVEL OF CHURCH INVOLVEMENT

	Visitor	Occasional Attendee (0–2 times monthly)	Regular attendee (3+ times monthly)	Member	I am serving on a ministry team	I am in a small group	I am leading a ministry team	Total
Q3: African American	6.99% 10	14.69% 21	50.35% 72	32.87% 47	17.48% 25	10.49% 15	1.40% 2	37.28% 192
Q3: Hispanic	2.02% 2	19.19% 19	54.55% 54	26.26% 26	11.11% 11	15.15% 15	3.03% 3	25.24% 130
Q3: Asian/Pacific Islander	9.72% 7	8.33% 6	51.39% 37	31.94% 23	19.44% 14	12.50% 9	4.17% 3	19.22% 99
Q3: Caucasian	2.56% 4	13.46% 21	51.92% 81	42.95% 67	25.00% 39	25.64% 40	5.13% 8	50.49% 260
Q3: Native American	0.00% 0	23.08% 3	46.15% 6	23.08% 3	23.08% 3	7.69% 1	0.00% 0	3.11% 16
Q3: African	0.00% 0	17.65% 3	41.18% 7	35.29% 6	23.53% 4	5.88% 1	0.00% 0	4.08% 21
Q3: Caribbean	25.00% 1	0.00% 0	50.00% 2	25.00% 1	0.00% 0	0.00% 0	0.00% 0	0.78% 4
Q3: Multiracial	3.57% 1	7.14% 2	64.29% 18	35.71% 10	14.29% 4	21.43% 6	10.71% 3	8.54% 44
Q3: Other	0.00% 0	20.00% 3	40.00% 6	46.67% 7	20.00% 3	20.00% 3	13.33% 2	4.66% 24
Total Respondents	24	75	263	182	97	85	20	515

To highlight the significance of what might seem like an insignificant discrepancy, consider the raw numbers of the respondents to this question in relation to the overall demographics of the church. Of the twenty total respondents who indicated participation at the ministry team leadership level, eight are Caucasian and only two are African American. Thus, while the overall percentage of Caucasian (30.4 percent) and African American (27.5 percent) congregants in the church is very similar,[9] the ratio of members in each group that hold formal leadership positions within the church is dramatically different. While Caucasians comprise 40 percent, African Americans comprise only 10 percent of the lay-team leaders in the church. This discrepancy is also highlighted when looking at the other two largest ethnic groups in the church—Hispanics and Asian/Pacific Islanders. While the representation of Hispanics (15 percent) and Asian/Pacific Islanders (15 percent) in leadership is higher than African Americans, they still fall significantly short of Caucasians. What becomes apparent, then, is that Caucasians are disproportionately represented in lay-leadership when compared with the other three main ethnic groups present in the church.

This hierarchy is not limited to lay-leaders, however. Four of the eight pastoral and ministry staff members at The Lighthouse are Caucasian, and all three of the executive pastoral leadership positions are held by Caucasians. Thus, the most influential paid ministry positions and half of all of the paid ministry positions in the church are held by Caucasian's, mirroring the imbalance displayed in lay-leadership positions as well. Together, this reveals a clear ethnic hierarchy within the polity and ministry structures of the church. While this hierarchy does not appear to be intentional or malicious in any way based on the data or my observations, it certainly has implications for the life and mission of the church, especially as it relates to the church's ability to engage its immediate community missionally.

Effects of The Lighthouse's Ethnic Hierarchy on Missional Participation

The negative effects of the ethnic hierarchy on the church's ability to engage its community through mission activities is illustrated by the data from my interview with Tina, one of the ethnic minority women on the pastoral staff team. While Tina is appreciative and positive toward the progress that has been made relating to ethnic diversity among the church leadership over the last few years, she also expressed frustration relating to how she perceived lingering issues relating to Caucasian leadership. When I asked her how

---

9. See Figure 2 in chapter 1.

the staff was doing relating to its mission focus and practices in relation to including people of color in the decisions, she noted that, "Things are improving, but still need a lot more work.... Some of the ways we do things, culturally speaking ... I would like to see more results than [us] just being here." She especially mentioned her frustration with how decisions were processed and made relating to the Community Center.

> It feels paternalistic, overall, rather than inclusive and participatory. The people in the community need more inclusion and ownership. ... I mean, opening the Drop-in Center between 10:00–2:00 is a waste; it is not a feasible hour. I don't know who made that decision, but many are still waking up in this neighborhood at that time. Well, OK, I'm pretty sure Pastor Peter made the decision, but I'm not sure who he consulted with about it. If he would have talked to one of us, I would have told him not to do it. We live in this neighborhood; we have a better idea what people need and want.

Tina continued communicating her frustrations with Pastor Peter, suggesting that someone who has been in this type of role before—or at least someone who was more familiar with the needs in the neighborhood—should be making decisions. "He needs help seeing what people need; to really hear the heart of the people. I don't know what the criteria is to decide, but the people maybe can help him see it." She compared the issue to missionaries who build a watering hole that they think African villagers need rather than a soccer field.

> If they would have asked the villagers what they needed, they would have expressed it to them. If we find common theme of what people need or are looking for, they would tell us. Give the community a place to come decide. Bring them together and then they can start talking, "Do we need a community watering hole?" Just ask them, "What do you need?" I'm not sure that we built the soccer field for our community; it is the watering hole that we wanted to provide. It is our idea of what the community needs rather than giving the community input. I mean, what do you really see that is relevant in the community? Gangs, substance abuse, and crime are big in our one-mile radius. Kids needing activities that will build into them positively in a safe space. What is the common theme that could have brought the community together? If we could have focused more on sports and activities where all can have input, it would have been better. Maybe a Twelve Step program. So right now, the village is being used, but the villagers are not coming.

Charismatic Leadership and Missional Change

Tina is highlighting the effects of both leadership schema that I have discussed in this chapter here—the top-down, clergy-centered approach to leadership, which causes the majority of decisions relating to the church's mission praxis to flow from the paid professionals down to lay-people, as well as the Euro-centric leadership schema that appears to be shaping the focus and method of mission in The Lighthouse's community. In this case, the effects of the combination of both schemas has created a high level of frustration for Tina because she feels that decisions—especially relating to the Community Center—are being made separate from the people that are most impacted by the center. The result is programs that are a waste of time and energy because they are having minimal impact on the people the programs are designed to serve. For Tina, the approach to decision-making feels paternalistic, and because of that, it misses the mark when it comes to programs being developed to impact the community.

Three other lay leaders and another ministry staff member all concurred with the feelings expressed by Tina, acknowledging that they see the top-down decision-making structures contributing toward a paternalistic posture in the community. Paul, who serves on the ministry staff, and Leroy took it a step further by connecting this paternalistic approach specifically to the perceived ethnic hierarchy in the church. Paul, for example, says:

> I like what's happened so far, but I hope the diversity issue continues to grow. The leadership and decisions are still made by white people—at least the big issues. We need an African American at the MSL level or higher. We need some diversity on our executive team. Right now, they are all white. I also get bothered in the service at times when predominantly white people are up front but you're talking multicultural. I know others who it bothers too. I have high hopes for what I see starting to happen, but there is still a long way to go.

Similarly, Leroy mentioned that he sees a low value for including people from the community and sometimes for having lay leaders in the church participate in decision-making processes because they do not "fit their idea of what makes a leader." In other words, they do not fit into the Euro-centric leadership schema that is valued by the senior Caucasian leaders. Consequently, when informants are sought across ethnic boundaries, they usually fit into this schema, which patently eliminates the voices of those who do not. Unfortunately, many people in the church and in the immediate community, especially those coming from outside Euro-centric culture backgrounds, often do not fit into this schema. This ultimately eliminates valuable voices that could potentially speak into the development of relevant programs and other mission initiatives in the community.

Pastor Steve also spoke to the importance of this issue indirectly, when I asked him where new ideas for missional initiatives come from within the congregation and how they are implemented. He noted his efforts to seek out diversity intentionally because of his concern that as a white male living in a neighborhood by the beach, he might not be the best person to have a pulse on the community. He states:

> I seek out diversity intentionally. I try to love and trust people no matter what color they are. I also try to communicate with cultural and gender sensitivity so that they feel accepted. This has become a growing priority for me over the past four or five years as we have become more diverse. I work more now to be inclusive. For example, I try to gain a Pacific Islander perspective, a street perspective, and youth perspective. I can only do that by engaging with people. What do Lynette, Karla, and Tina have to say? Things are more and more complex. Fun, but a lot more work.

What is important to note here is that while his intentionality is commendable, the people he mentions as informants are all on his staff in some capacity and fit into the Euro-centric leadership schema that he and the executive leadership team value. While these are likely not his only informants, it is revealing that these individuals are those he mentioned when asked.

This issue is not isolated to Pastor Steve, however, and may extend to the other Caucasian executive team members as well. All four of the executive members, who are Caucasian, live at least five miles away from the church and its surrounding community. And while each said that they try to utilize informants when making programming decisions, it is possible that they are also approaching informants who fit into their Euro-centric leadership schema. This might ultimately prevent them from talking with the diverse cultural voices necessary to give them the insights they need to make well-informed decisions relating to missions initiatives in the community. Pastor Peter, for example, mentioned four key informants during our interview, and of those he mentioned, all fit into his definition of sharp. My observations in staff meetings and my interactions with each of these leaders also seems to verify this interpretation, as the names given to me by these leaders as informants and the individuals I saw them regularly interacting with seemed to fit into the values shaping their leadership schema. Thus, while Pastor Steve and the pastoral staff's efforts are commendable and a step in the right direction, Pastor Steve acknowledges that they also seem to fall short of what is necessary to see beyond, and potentially re-shape, the dominant culture's leadership schema that is shaping the mission praxis of the church.

SUMMARY

In this discussion, I have highlighted three adaptive challenges facing the church in light of the top-down, charismatic approach to leadership employed at the church: (1) a gap between a lived and preferred value for missional in the congregation; (2) the congregation's over-dependence on the charismatic leader; and (3) the way a Euro-centric leadership schema is shaping leadership selection and development by the staff. Throughout this discussion, I have demonstrated how these adaptive challenges—along with the leadership schemas informing them—have hindered, and will likely continue to hinder, missional participation, innovation, and creativity among the ethnically diverse people of God in The Lighthouse. Because of this, I suggest that the top-down charismatic model of leadership that has built up and sustained the church to this point can only hold it back if leadership does not adapt new values and practices. A charismatic leadership model, which is well suited for an attractional model of ministry, cannot keep up with the trajectory toward missional because it is geared toward carrying out the vision of the leader rather than facilitating missional participation and innovation among the people. Instead, I suggest that pastoral leadership needs to give the work back to the people by shaping an interpretive community that can tap into the collective, Spirit-led wisdom of the everyday people of God. Doing this, I suggest, will help create an environment that can foster missional innovation throughout the congregation and ultimately help to create a more sustainable long-term approach. In the next chapter, then, I will explore this claim as I reflect on the issues missiologically.

5

Missiological Implications of the Leadership Praxis at The Lighthouse

IN VARIOUS PARTS OF this book, I have offered a critique of charismatic, top-down, leader-centric models of leadership in The Lighthouse and other Christian congregations. I have suggested instead that what is needed at The Lighthouse is a more participatory approach that creates environments for the everyday people of God to discern God's initiatives in their community. It is important to note that I make this suggestion not simply because the approach is a more culturally appropriate form of leadership for the post-modern context in the United States. Instead, I suggest it because it is a form of ministry leadership grounded in the narratives of the early church that seems particularly appropriate for the complex ministry environment that leaders of The Lighthouse—and those of other multiethnic congregations—currently find themselves in.

In this chapter, then, I will invite the larger Christian story to speak into the leadership praxis at The Lighthouse. To carry out this task, I will briefly survey two key Lukan narratives, Acts 10–15 and Luke 10:1–24, that portray a picture of God's people participating in his missional initiatives in specific contexts. Within this discussion, I will illustrate four missional priorities defined by Mark Lau Branson that flow directly from the narratives.[1] I will then reflect on the leadership praxis at The Lighthouse in light of these priorities in order to illustrate how effectively pastoral leadership at The Lighthouse is currently living into them. This will allow me to then

1. Branson, "Perspectives."

Charismatic Leadership and Missional Change

draw inferences into how leaders of other multiethnic congregations might shape missional praxis among their diverse followers.

MISSIONAL LIFE IN LUKE/ACTS

According to Luke Timothy Johnson, the narrative contained in Acts 10–15 is a pivotal episode in the book of Acts as well as in God's salvation history. It presents perhaps one of the clearest and most pertinent examples of God's ongoing redemptive activity in the world and the church's invitation to participate in it. It is here that the church in Jerusalem answers the questions of whether the conversion of the Gentiles was legitimate or not, and if so, on what grounds they would be considered part of God's people.[2]

Beginning in Acts 10, the episode features two visions from God: the first to a Roman centurion living in Caesarea named Cornelius (Acts 10:1–8), who is described as devout, God-fearing, and generous; and, the second to the apostle Peter the following day in Joppa during his prayer time (10:9–20). These visions—both cryptic and incomplete—lead Peter to follow Cornelius's messengers to Caesarea with lots of uncertainty (10:21–23), where: (1) he will listen to Cornelius's story to more fully discern how God is at work in the situation; (2) he will preach the Gospel to Cornelius and his entire household (10:24–43); (3) this Gentile family will receive the Gospel and experience a second Pentecost experience as the Holy Spirit is poured out on them (10:44–46); and (4) they will subsequently be baptized as Peter more fully understands God's missional agenda to the Gentiles (10:47–48). This, of course, leads to controversy in the Jerusalem church, as the Jewish believers criticize Peter for violating their long held ethnocentric and exclusivist understanding of God's mission in the world and their customs relating to their ritual purity (11:1–2, 18).[3]

Through the subsequent public discourse (11:3–18), Peter shares how God poured his Spirit out on the Gentiles when they believed, to fulfill both the vision God provided (11:4–10) and the promise of Jesus (11:16). This leads the gathered church to discern and recognize the legitimacy of God's salvific work among the Gentiles (11:18), and moves the church into a new and unprecedented phase of mission to the Gentiles (11:19–14:28). This sparks a second controversy pertaining to Gentile inclusion into the people of God, specifically relating to their willingness to adhere to Jewish covenant rituals. Through a lengthy process of

2. Johnson, *Scripture and Discernment*, 89.
3. Johnson, *Scripture and Discernment*, 97.

communal discernment involving public speech, dialogue, theologizing, and prayer, this issue is also settled (15:1–21). The Gentiles are granted full and equal inclusion into the people of God without adherence to the Jewish customs and rituals that had characterized their religious life for centuries, except those that will permit them to participate in table fellowship with the Jewish believers (15:23–31).[4]

Luke's account of Jesus's sending of the seventy[5] (Luke 10:1–24) provides a different, yet, complimentary reading to the Acts 10–15 narrative. In this passage, we see Jesus send out his disciples in pairs ahead of him to the nearby towns to proclaim the arrival of the Kingdom of God (Luke 10:1–9). He sends them out in a posture of vulnerability (10:3), and instructs them to take nothing with them that can sustain them (10:4). Instead, he instructs them to seek out individuals and households who will extend them hospitality (10:5–7). Whether someone in the home is receptive to their message or not, they are to remain with them, eating and drinking whatever is set before them (10:6–7). They should then proclaim and embody the Good News for as long as the town they are in remains receptive and hospitable (10:8–9). When a town rejects them, however, He instructs them to move on (10:10–16). The story then culminates with the disciples returning with good reports full of joy because of how God moved through them (10:17), and with Jesus listening to their stories, instructing them, and celebrating what God has done through them (10:18–24).

Together, these rich and detailed narratives provide several valuable insights into the missional life and practices of the early New Testament church. These insights in turn inform four specific priorities that leaders of multiethnic congregations can live into to lead their people into more faithful expressions of Gospel life and mission in their communities. Together, they also provide a framework to reflect missiologically on the leadership praxis at The Lighthouse.

Discerning God's Initiatives in Context

In both passages, we see that God's people discern God's initiatives in relationships with ordinary people in homes and public spaces outside the walls of the synagogue and church. In Peter's case, with Cornelius and his

---

4. Johnson, *Scripture and Discernment*, 104.

5. Some translations, such as CEV, ESV, and NIV, record seventy-two disciples rather than seventy.

messengers.[6] In the case of the seventy, with the families they stayed with and likely in village gathering places.[7] In both cases, we see that the Spirit of God is the primary agent of mission, working on the ground ahead of the church. In the Acts narrative, the sequencing of the visions highlights that God is already working in the lives of Cornelius and those in his household.[8] In Luke, it is implied that God is already at work in the people of peace who receive the disciples, and among those they will interact with in the villages in their gatherings and public spaces.[9]

According to Mark Branson, then, leaders in local congregations need to place a priority on discerning God's initiatives in their contexts. This conveys a simple yet often missed missiological truth concerning the church's participation in the *missio Dei*—mission is and always has been God's endeavor in the world that he has graciously invited his church into.[10] This understanding carries the belief that God is alive and active in local communities across the globe, and therefore it is the responsibility of local churches in those contexts to seek out, discern, and participate with God in his redemptive initiatives in those contexts. It is not up to those churches to start such initiatives on their own based solely off of biblical commands, expert strategies, or the vision of a leader. Rather, the priority of those leading such churches needs to radically shift from relying on expert strategies seeking "to present religious goods and services to their neighbors ... that have worked in other contexts,"[11] to discerning God's initiatives on the ground through personal and corporate practices such as mutual hospitality, scripture meditation, and prayer.

Treating Neighbors as Subject/Agents

Luke also prioritizes a second practice in both of his narratives—entering into relationships characterized by mutuality. In the Acts narrative, we see that because Peter treats Cornelius and his messengers as equals in their relationship, significant learning occurs in both parties. Luke's narrative here

---

6. Johnson, *Scripture and Discernment*, 107.
7. Roxburgh, *Missional*, 146.
8. Johnson, *Scripture and Discernment*.
9. Roxburgh, *Missional*, 142–48.
10. See Moltmann, *Church in the Power*, 64; Van Gelder and Zscheile, *Missional Church*, 4.
11. Branson, "Perspectives," 37–38.

reveals that Peter and Cornelius's stories actually interpret each other.[12] In the Luke 10 story, Jesus places his disciples in a state of dependence on those they will receive hospitality from when he tells them to leave their bags behind (10:4). By instructing them to remain in the homes of the people they would be visiting (10:5), they gain access to family and village life, which will be essential to carrying out their mission effectively.[13]

What this suggests, then, according to Branson, is that churches need to treat their neighbors as subject/agents rather than objects of their missions activities as they participate with God in his redemptive initiatives.[14] This understanding views people as active participants in God's activities in a given context rather than passive spectators. Accordingly, people and leaders in local churches need to be connected in relationships with real people in order to discern how God is already moving among them.[15] This requires a shift for churches used to providing predetermined structures and programs or that have relied on expert strategies to reach their neighbors absent of relationship and on the ground knowledge. This over-reliance on universals over the particular tends to desensitize churches regarding the lives and voices of their neighbors in a given local context and often results in churches that are increasingly out of touch with what the Spirit of God is doing in their local contexts. The result is objectification over relationship, and such approaches keep those on the outside, outside.[16]

Crossing Boundaries

"People like to become Christians without crossing racial, linguistic, or class barriers."[17] This descriptive statement—known in missiology as the homogeneous unit principle—was developed through the missionary experience and field research conducted by Donald McGavran among the caste system in India in the fifties and sixties. It was later refined and applied prescriptively to congregational mission efforts in the United States by those in the Church Growth Movement[18] and popularized by mega-church pastors like

---

12. Johnson, *Scripture and Discernment*, 107.
13. Roxburgh, *Missional*, 137.
14. Roxburgh, *Missional*, 38.
15. Warnes, "Shifting Perceptions," 20.
16. Warnes, "Shifting Perceptions," 15–22.
17. McGavran and Wagner, *Understanding Church Growth*, 163.
18. McGavran and Wagner, *Understanding Church Growth*, 163.

Rick Warren[19] and Bill Hybels. To ease the task of evangelism and to grow larger churches faster, they suggested, we should seek to primarily reach people like us, thus removing uncomfortable social barriers that might cause people anxiety and hinder the spread of the Gospel.[20]

We see a different approach in both Lukan narratives, however. Instead, crossing socio-cultural and religious boundaries seems to be an important part of joining God in his redemptive initiatives in a given social context. In the Acts narrative, Peter crosses taboo social and religious boundaries to discern how God is already working among the Gentile Cornelius and his household.[21] While not as clear, Jesus's counsel for his disciples to eat and drink whatever their hosts set before them also suggests the possibility of crossing a social taboo (Luke 10:7).

According to Branson, then, faithfully participating in God's mission necessarily involves prioritizing boundary crossing.[22] Generally speaking, this requires a significant shift for leaders and people in local congregations alike, as people generally do not like to cross boundaries that make us uncomfortable. When we do need to cross these boundaries, we prefer situations that we can control, so that we can retreat to safety when things get too difficult or challenging. In the Incarnation, however, Jesus models a different way. He embodies the ultimate boundary-crossing nature of the Gospel as he crosses the divine/human boundary to make his dwelling among us (John 1:14). In doing so, he invites us to follow him in ways that are risky, but ultimately necessary, if we are to faithfully and fully live into Gospel life characterized by reconciliation and *shalom*.

Shaping Environments through Plural Leadership

Finally, in both passages, leaders shape environments where God's people can discern God's initiatives together. In Luke 10, Jesus provides an environment for his disciples to share and reflect on what they have learned from the relationships they have formed on the ground so that their learning will inform their praxis moving forward (10:17–24). In the Acts narrative, the apostles and elders together shape an environment where the

---

19. See Warren, *Purpose Driven Church*.
20. Wagner, *Church Growth*.
21. Wagner, *Church Growth*, 107.
22. Branson, "Perspectives," 39–41.

collective people of God can discern God's larger missional agenda with the Gentiles (Acts 11; 15).[23]

Branson's fourth priority, then, runs counter to prevailing ideas of the leader as hero or expert. It suggests instead that Spirit-led leadership for communities of faith happens most effectively when a plurality of leaders shape environments where the people of God can collectively discern how God might be inviting them to participate in his initiatives among them.[24] While current approaches that emphasize the gifts, strengths, and understanding of a single leader are appealing because of their promise to provide certainty and solutions to problems that people are facing, they ultimately fall short because they rely on one person to discern God's activities in a given context. This approach implicitly denies that the Spirit of God is at work among various people in a congregation,[25] and ultimately mitigates the collective gifts and wisdom of the people of God. A plurality of leaders who are shaping environments where people can share life and discern God's initiatives together can instead release "the missional imagination of God's ordinary people"[26] and move them towards faithful participation in Gospel life together.

DISCERNING GOD'S INITIATIVES AT THE LIGHTHOUSE

In light of the way we see God at work redemptively in the public spaces in the Lukan narratives above, it seems fair to suggest that Spirit-led leadership needs to be about forming churches that can discern and participate more fully in God's initiatives in their particular contexts.[27] The problem according to Dwight Zscheile, however, is that our current models of leadership in the church are inspired more by American cultural values of individualism, self-reliance, and heroic ideas of leadership than they are by Trinitarian approaches emphasizing collaboration and listening together in community. What we often see, then, are solitary approaches toward visioning God's will where the job of the leader is to discern God's vision privately, then dictate it to the community of faith in a clear and compelling way. The problem with this approach—as we see in Peter's encounter

23. Johnson, *Scripture and Discernment*.
24. Branson, "Perspectives," 41.
25. Branson, "Perspectives," 41–42.
26. Roxburgh and Romanuk, *Missional Leader*, 29.
27. Branson, "Ecclesiology and Leadership," 118–19.

Charismatic Leadership and Missional Change

with Cornelius and in the disciples' encounters in public spaces and the homes of their neighbors—is that God's vision and call often come from unexpected places on the margins rather than centers of power.[28] In light of this, Zscheile suggests that leaders need to shift the emphasis from discerning in solitude to creating spaces where collaborative dialogue and listening can occur, such as what occurred in the Jerusalem Council (Acts 15). Similar to Peter and James's roles in both collective gatherings discussed previously, leadership becomes more about communicating "how God is at work in our midst, framing past, present, and future reality in light of God's redemptive history and promises."[29]

In light of this understanding, how might we assess The Lighthouse's commitment to living into this missional priority of discerning God's initiatives? In short, the top-down, charismatic approach toward leadership at The Lighthouse is currently hindering their ability to live into this priority well. Living more fully into this priority will require a transformation of the clergy-centered and Euro-centric leadership schemas that are shaping congregational life and mission.

Joining God or Bringing God to the Neighborhood?

Reflecting on my findings and the theological reflections just presented, it seems apparent that The Lighthouse's posture more closely resembles bringing God to the neighborhood than joining him where he is already at work. While there have certainly been attempts to discern where God is at work, such as a community survey carried out by the community center taskforce and the occasional use of cultural informants by Pastor Steve and other paid staff, these attempts have been isolated at best. And often when they did occur, the results were ignored or set aside by the paid professionals. The incidents described earlier with the community center taskforce are a prime example of this. The computer training afterschool program and the drop-in center were initiated by the paid staff member overseeing the team but independent of the collected data and against the opinions of the taskforce. They were initiated out of a perceived opportunity by one individual rather than by an intentional analysis of how God was already involved in the neighborhood. As such, the programs appeared to be more about offering religious goods and services to the church's customers than joining in partnership with God and neighbor.

28. Zscheile, *Agile Church*, 60.
29. Zscheile, *Agile Church*, 61.

Missiological Implications of the Leadership Praxis at The Lighthouse

Further, as I discussed in chapter 4, an overwhelming majority of mission initiatives that have been launched over the last several years have been launched by the paid pastors and ministry staff leaders. According to their own words during interviews, these initiatives were launched based either on courses they have taken, conferences they have attended, books they have read, expert strategies they have learned, or needs they have perceived in the congregation and/or neighborhood in consultation with one another. Rather than creating environments where they can come together with other congregants and/or their neighbors to discern where God is already at work so that they can join in, the majority of congregants remain on the sidelines as the paid staff do the work of discernment, decision making, and innovation. Annual events, such as Church Without Walls, Bible Fiesta Fun, and Serve Day, along with ongoing ministries, such as new church services, the community garden, and MECA, are offered to the neighborhood based off perceived need rather than through a deep engagement with those in the community and the congregation. Instead, lay members are recruited after the fact, utilizing programs like the Volunteer Service Core to fill volunteer needs to ensure that the programs can function the way they are intended.

The clergy-centered leadership schema feeds directly into this top-down approach at The Lighthouse and serves to center the work of discernment and decision making away from those who are interpersonally connected with people in the neighborhood. The Euro-centric leadership schema shaped by modern management frameworks also contributes to this tendency, as it filters out those who might offer the most insight into opportunities and needs in the neighborhood or opportunities for partnerships where God is already at work. This runs counter to the practices that I highlighted in the Lukan narratives above. In both narratives, a large part of the discernment process was carried out by God's people on the ground as they engaged in relationships outside the walls of the church. Further, in the Acts narrative, while the apostles and elders drove the process, it is clear that the entire congregation was involved in the discernment process at some level (Acts 15). There was an iterative process that occurred over time, where leaders and members alike were able to engage communally in discourse, prayer, and scripture interpretation to discern together where God was at work and how he was inviting them to join him.

Charismatic Leadership and Missional Change

Individual or Corporate Leadership Praxis?

Roxburgh and Romanuk suggest that missional innovation occurs in congregations as leaders cultivate dialogue and listening across the system. Conversely, when leaders rely on their own discernment and ability to interpret the situation, they thwart creativity and innovation among their followers because they create dependency on their plans and leadership.[30] This perspective sums up the approach at The Lighthouse quite well.

Through the observations and interviews conducted during my research, I was unable to discern any environments (construction sites) created by the staff where missional ideas held by congregants could be uncovered and nurtured. I was also unable to uncover any construction sites where corporate reflection and discernment were occurring beyond individual theological reflection engaged in by leaders. Rather than consistently engaging in corporate interpretive work in construction sites to shape their mission praxis, the data shows that the paid professionals at The Lighthouse tend to rely on their own skills and abilities to provide people in the congregation and in the neighborhood with what they believe they need. Consequently, while there appears to be a good deal of theological reflection engaged in by particular leaders on their own ministry practice, there are no spaces to engage in corporate reflection, dialogue, and prayer that lead toward new mission praxis among the congregation. Beyond simple debriefings after events in staff meetings, there also appeared to be few, if any, spaces to engage in reflection as a staff. In the current leadership model at The Lighthouse, this type of process appears to be absent. Serious reflection on mission praxis is carried out almost exclusively by Pastor Steve and, in increasing frequency, by the Senior Executive team.

This approach runs contrary to the model presented by the early Jerusalem church and ultimately carries inherent challenges with it regarding discernment and missional innovation in the congregation. Because it centers interpretive work and the power for discernment and decision making with the paid professionals and experts, it hinders missional identity formation in the everyday people of God. This has undoubtedly contributed toward the gap between lived and espoused values for mission-actional in the congregation and has thwarted missional innovation on the margins. As the neighborhood continues to change around it, it is likely that this will create more challenges, as those most connected to the neighborhood are marginalized in the church's discernment processes. It has also

---

30. Roxburgh and Romanuk, *Missional Leader*, 26–35.

likely continued to reinforce the clergy-centered leadership schema that is shaping the mission praxis at the church, which ultimately strengthens the adaptive challenge faced by the congregation regarding over-dependence on the charismatic leader.

In contradistinction to the current approach to discernment at The Lighthouse, Dwight Zscheile offers some appropriate thoughts. He suggests that a Trinitarian approach shifts the focus of leadership from seeking God's will in solitude to framing an environment where the congregation can discern where God is at work in their midst in light of his redemptive history and promises. He posits that "the Trinity offers a rich symbol for considering how communities can come together in reciprocal, collaborative dialogue for transformation and discovery."[31] Discerning God's initiatives in this sense, then, is not just about interpreting reality for others. Instead,

> it involves a deep, relational conversation of listening and speaking in which all parties risk learning as well as changing. Leaders then have the opportunity and challenge of creating spaces for authentic, mutual conversation among and with members of the church. For pastors used to being the experts who hold the answers, this may represent a major redefinition of role.[32]

While this shift in role is not easy, it is necessary if The Lighthouse desires to move more faithfully into Gospel life and mission in its neighborhood as a community of interpreters that can respond to God's gracious invitation to join him where He is already at work.

TREATING NEIGHBORS AS SUBJECTS AT THE LIGHTHOUSE

Since the increase in popularity of the Church Growth Movement[33] in the nineties, local congregations have increasingly depended on demographic studies, transferable ministry models based on universal principles of church growth, and identifying and meeting the needs of a defined target audience through customized programs to engage their contexts.[34] Due to their impersonal, universalistic, and programmed approaches, these ministries

---

31. Zscheile, "Trinity," 60.
32. Zscheile, "Trinity," 61.
33. See McGavran and Wagner, *Understanding Church Growth*; Wagner, *Church Growth*; Rainer, *Book of Church Growth*; Barna, *Grow Your Church*.
34. See Warren, *Purpose Driven Church*.

Charismatic Leadership and Missional Change

primarily operate from a subject-object paradigm where religious goods and services are provided to religious consumers. The problem with this type of approach is that it creates controlled environments and packaged programs that distance both leaders and everyday people in the church from their neighbors. With the experts providing all of the vital services that their ministry targets need, people are limited in their options for involvement. While some may choose to volunteer in programs and provide financial support, others may decide to sit a back, watch, and consume the provisions. Ministry becomes the task of the paid professional, and vital points of contact with their neighbors are slowly cut off. Over time, the church misses out on the real-life stories of people in their community and lose touch with how God is already at work in and among their neighbors.

Those in the missional church discussion have worked to counter those trends, however, seeking to move churches toward incarnational approaches to ministry that operate from a subject-subject paradigm. This development has been encouraging, as it has moved leaders and congregants alike into more vulnerable and genuine, life-on-life encounters with their neighbors where they can sense God's Spirit at work. Just as Peter and Cornelius's stories actually interpret one another and Jesus's disciples enter into vulnerable relationships of mutuality with their neighbors, it is through encounters with neighbors as subject/agents where people in the church learn "how God is present, what opportunities exist for partnerships, and how a church can participate in healing, beauty, trust-building, belonging and witness."[35] When we truly engage our neighbors as subjects, giving them agency in God's initiatives as well, then our expectations and behaviors shift in new directions. When we stop relying solely on collecting data and predetermined programs, we begin to learn how to walk alongside them in mutuality, vulnerability, and giving and receiving hospitality as we seek God's peace together (Luke 10:6–7; Jer 29:7).

As I previously discussed, while The Lighthouse has a long way to go living into this priority, it has made some strides in this area. As the focus of The Lighthouse's mission efforts has continued to shift towards its one-mile radius, there has been a greater concern and compassion demonstrated toward her neighbors. However, because the posture of the church is still primarily about bringing God to the neighborhood rather than joining God in what He is doing, there is still a tendency to see people in the surrounding neighborhood as objects of mission rather than as subjects.

---

35. Branson, "Perspectives," 38–39.

Rather than engaging in relationships of mutuality and hospitality, The Lighthouse primarily seeks to engage its community through programs and events. Rather than promoting innovation on the margins among the everyday people of God, innovation tends to be top-down, engaged in primarily by the paid professionals. Because of this, true spiritual, relational, and economic impact has not been as significant as it might be.

Seeking God's Peace through Programs and Control

The unmet potential of The Lighthouse's mission efforts are explained in part by the gap between a lived and preferred value for missional that exists among leaders and the congregation. Another likely reason, however, is the church's lack of a truly incarnational presence in the community. While the community center is intended to meet that goal, it still primarily functions as a hub designed to draw people in by providing services for them rather than extending the grace of God outward as an incarnational presence in partnership. This ecclesio-centric approach to mission limits the church's ability to discern the initiatives that God might be inviting them to join him in with their neighbors. Unlike Peter in the Acts narrative, leaders and congregants are not engaged in the types of relationships that allow them to mutually interpret what the Holy Spirit may be already doing.

The current ministry environment is due in large part to the centralized control of decision-making surrounding programming flowing from the clergy-centered ministry schema. But it is also due to the fact that the mission praxis of the church is still heavily centered on annual, one-time events and service projects rather than ongoing relationships and process. This focus on event over relationship and process has hindered the church from entering into relationships with their neighbors characterized by mutuality and mutual hospitality. What this has practically served to do, then, is eliminate voices from the church's neighbors in any of the decision-making processes surrounding mission efforts in their community. Instead, decision-making is centered on a few—most often the paid experts—who dictate what programs and services are offered to and for the community, rather than with it.

This emphasis on events flows directly from Pastor Steve's own personal bias toward crisis and event-oriented evangelism over longer, relational, and process-oriented forms of outreach as revealed in his interview data earlier. This bias was revealed by his expressed concern over church finances as well as his desire to see quicker numerical growth from events.

Charismatic Leadership and Missional Change

These concerns reveal his ecclesio-centric focus, which ultimately dictate the church's mission praxis.[36] Processes, programs, and even relational approaches to ministry that take too long, that might consume too many resources, or that negatively impact the financial bottom line without contributing toward numerical growth that will sustain the church, are filtered out. In this, we see how Pastor Steve is making his way reflexively through his ministry environment. He is carefully weighing his ultimate concerns relating to financial viability and numerical growth against a shift to more incarnational and relationally focused ministry. In the end, his ultimate concerns prevail, and he continues to promote and support events and programs that the church can control and that have more tangible outcomes. Ultimately, shifting fully into the types of relationships that move control away from the centers of power in the church seems too risky, and in light of Pastor Steve's concerns, unlikely.

Innovation from the Top Down

In chapter 4, I highlighted that almost all innovation at The Lighthouse's is top-down, driven by the pastoral staff. That is, rather than missional innovation and creativity occurring among the everyday people of God on the margins of church life and among their neighbors, new mission initiatives tend to be driven by the paid pastoral and ministry staff. This, again, is informed by the clergy-centered ministry schema that shapes the mission praxis of the church and ensures a level of professionalism, control, and, ideally, success that is expected. As the church is still heavily oriented around Sunday services, ministries, and mid-week programs offered in the church building, most of these programs are staff-led because of the expectation for quality and excellence. New programs and ministries are, for the most part, also expected to be initiated by staff, because that is what they are paid to do.

This does not mean that lay-people cannot begin new ministries, however. My research revealed that there have been small groups and particular ministries in the church—such as the Volunteer Service Corps—started by lay leaders. What it does mean is that approval and support is obtained through a rigorous process with the paid staff. And for a new initiative to be approved, the leader/s will need to be approved. This, I believe, is where another subtle inhibitor gets in the way of innovation on

---

36. Roxburgh, *Missional*, 92.

the margins. Prospective leaders need to fit criteria of leadership that has been established in the church, and that ultimately affects leadership selection. This is where the Euro-centric leadership schema held and shaped by the Caucasian ministry staff has a perceived affect as well. People from other cultural backgrounds in the church, who might connect best with the church's diverse neighbors, don't always fit the correct criteria for leadership as determined by this schema. The consequence is that many people who are living incarnationally among their neighbors have had their role unintentionally relegated to that of inviting their neighbor to church to hear the Gospel from the paid professional or to another program designed to meet their needs.

This unintended consequence, I believe, has hindered The Lighthouse's ability to promote and sustain missional innovation on the margins because decisions are kept in the centers of power and disconnected from those with the most pertinent relational and cultural information. This has served to reinforce cycles of dependency on the paid professionals, centering agency among the pastoral staff. Valuable voices among the everyday people of God who are vitally connected in relationships with their neighbors have been cut-off, and the interpretive capacity of the congregation has therefore been diminished.

A Pathway Toward Subject-Subject Ministry at The Lighthouse

For The Lighthouse to continue on its journey from attractional toward missional, it needs to live more fully into the priority of neighbor as subject. The problem, however, is that the current ministry and leadership schemas informing the mission praxis at The Lighthouse fight against this movement. They have instead locked the church into its current ecclesio-centric, mission-actional approach because the types of relationships necessary to see missional creativity and innovation occur on the margins, with their neighbors largely absent. The leadership model at The Lighthouse that centers on the influence of the charismatic leader actually thwarts creativity and innovation because it puts a straight-jacket around leaders and members who are now tied to the plan and dependent upon the leader.[37] It centers control among the paid professionals, who happen to be those with the least amount of relational contact with the church's neighbors. It also places

---

37. Roxburgh and Romanuk, *Missional Leader*, 26–27.

an emphasis on programs and events that ultimately treat The Lighthouse's neighbors as objects of mission rather than subjects.

For this trend to reverse, for The Lighthouse to live more fully into this priority, it will take an important shift. It will take a commitment from leadership to intentionally cultivate environments—construction sites—where listening can occur across the system. This listening attends to God through prayer and scripture, to their own experiences, and to their neighbors. It will take creating spaces where storytelling, listening, and peer learning can take place across and in spite of differences.[38] In our time-burdened culture, it may also mean lessening burdens on members' time by potentially offering fewer ministries that require them to volunteer. Ultimately, members need more time to invest in their neighbors relationally in ways that foster mutuality and trust. This can't happen when members are expected to constantly participate in, support, and volunteer for events and programs that exhaust their time and energy. This is risky, to be sure, but likely necessary if The Lighthouse is to move into a subject-subject posture with her neighbors.

BOUNDARY CROSSING AT THE LIGHTHOUSE

By pushing Peter across an uncomfortable and taboo social boundary in his encounter with Cornelius and his household, the Acts 10–15 narrative reinforces a clear pattern in scripture—God intends for his people to cross uncomfortable boundaries as we seek to live out Gospel life and participate in God's mission with our neighbors (Gen 12:1–3; Matt 28:19–20; Mark 16:15–16; Luke 10:25–37; John 4; Acts 1:8; 8:26–40; 10:1–15:35). Yet, in spite of recent trends that show an increase in the number of multiethnic churches, the overwhelming majority of local churches in contemporary American society remain ethnically homogeneous.[39] Paul Metzger highlights the crux of this problem, suggesting that both in the ways churches market and structure themselves and in the ways Christians make choices regarding the churches they attend, the consumer spirit so characteristic of the larger American culture is in fact deeply entrenched in the soul of American evangelicalism.[40] It is demonstrated in the ways churches cater to "church-shoppers," who want what they want, when they want it, through a message of self-gratification and fulfillment to the individual and an endless array of programmatic choices that draw in hungry consumers. The result

38. Zscheile, *Agile Church*, 125.
39. Emerson, *People of the Dream*.
40. Metzger, *Consuming Jesus*, 97.

has been a voluntary segregation "based on the norms of consumer preference" that has contributed toward a "homogeneous-unit-principled, safe-haven church where a family-friendly faith protects Christ's followers from those who think, look, and even sound different than they do."[41]

Living into the value of boundary crossing, then, is a significant adaptive challenge requiring leaders and congregants alike to learn new values, skills, and practices. Instead of functioning as closed communities that are only open to "people like us," people in local churches need to learn how to "reach across the chasm of cultural difference in ways that are loving and respectful"[42]—both inside and outside of the church. Branson suggests that this difficult work requires leaders to "weave new relational networks within the church and with neighbors . . . [for the purpose of] creating new contexts for speaking and listening."[43] Doing so can help to create new generative dialogues that are conducive to moving the congregation deeper into love and reconciliation with one another and with their neighbors. Together, they can discern the shape of Gospel life as they live in the midst of diverse people and ethnicities, learning new ways to discern and participate with God's initiatives in their community and beyond.

As a church that has become increasingly diverse, both ethnically and culturally, The Lighthouse has worked hard to live into this priority of boundary crossing. During the course of its journey, from a primarily Caucasian church engaging in attractional ministry toward becoming an extremely diverse church engaging in mission-actional ministry, The Lighthouse has become extremely diverse. For example, as I highlighted earlier, no single ethnic group in the church comprises more than 30.5 percent of the total attendance, and there are four different groups that comprise at least 15 percent. Further, as evidenced by the multicultural worship service held in 2009, there are no less than thirty different heart languages represented in the church. The church has also made some progress in staff hires, as half of the paid ministry staff now consists of ethnic minorities. Although this does not undo the critique offered previously relating to the presence of an ethnic hierarchy in the church, it does reflect a level of intentionality that was missing in Pastor Steve's earlier years of ministry there. This intentionality is reflected in Steve's current relational network, as he

---

41. Metzger, *Consuming Jesus*, 27.
42. Livermore, *Cultural Intelligence*, 13.
43. Branson, "Ecclesiology and Leadership," 121.

has also cultivated a diverse network of friends, informants, and cultural mentors that serve as a source of growth and learning for him.

Overall, the efforts at boundary crossing that The Lighthouse have taken are admirable, with the ethnic diversity in the church representing the diverse community that she finds herself in well. Considering where the church came from, as a primarily Caucasian church in decline, its multiethnic identity and growth is remarkable. Where the church still needs to grow, however, is in weaving diverse relational networks together where the nature of Gospel life can be discerned and shaped.[44]

In spite of the diversity at The Lighthouse, there appears to be a lack of meaningful relationships across these boundaries on several fronts. While there are certainly individual leaders and congregants who have friends across ethnic lines, these seem to be the exception rather than the rule. Through my observations and experiences, the ethnic diversity seems to manifest itself most clearly on Sundays, during worship services, and on some of the ministry teams rather than in small groups or personal friendships. On one front, this should not be entirely surprising since the Sunday focus and large event outreach orientation fights against involvement in the more intimate spheres of church life. For example, only 16.3 percent of respondents indicated involvement in a small group at all. Since some of these small groups are primarily homogeneous due to pre-existing friendship circles, opportunities for this type of relational involvement across boundaries are minimal in the existing church structure. This does not fully explain this phenomenon, however. It is highly likely that many congregants like the idea of diversity and boundary crossing, but their ultimate concerns for safety and stress management mitigate their actions.

Due to the fact that The Lighthouse is situated in the American sociocultural mission context, it is a fair assumption that it is impacted by the same cultural forces discussed earlier in this chapter. Further, because crossing racial and cultural boundaries raises discomfort and anxiety among particular groups of people in the racialized American social structure,[45] it is also a fair assumption to suggest that even in diverse church settings, many congregants will look to alleviate that anxiety whenever possible. Because large group settings like The Lighthouse's Sunday services primarily provide one-way dialogue from the pulpit, corporate prayer, and worship, there is a much lower level of intimacy. Similarly,

44. Branson, "Ecclesiology and Leadership," 121.
45. Tatum, *Black Kids*; DiAngelo, "White Fragility."

because of the task-oriented nature of most of the ministry teams, opportunities for meaningful relational engagement are minimized in these settings as well. Because of this, both of these ministry environments lower anxiety by providing a level of safety for those who do not desire to cross uncomfortable boundaries interpersonally due to the low level of commitment involved when the boundaries are crossed in this environment. Yet, at the same time, participants can feel good that they are present worshipping or serving with other diverse congregants. Conversely, more intimate settings, like small groups and one-on-one relationships, demand a much higher level of interpersonal engagement, which puts participants in a much more vulnerable space. Since these types of programs are not required of attendees, it is much easier for those who are still attending the church as religious consumers to opt out.

This discussion is symptomatic of the larger issue at The Lighthouse. While particular leaders and congregants do engage in meaningful relationships across racial, cultural, and class boundaries, my observations and informal discussions with many diverse members before and during the course of my research suggests that this type of interaction appears to be more limited in the larger body of the church as a whole. When you factor in relationships with diverse neighbors, this interaction appears to be even more limited. Accordingly, if The Lighthouse desires to more fully live into this priority in a way that invites Gospel *shalom* into their communal life and mission together, the church's posture and priorities need to shift. Less emphasis needs to be placed on events and more on process. Relational webs of connectedness need to be formed in construction sites where listening across the system can occur.[46]

Safe spaces need to be created where leaders, congregants, and neighbors can engage in ongoing conversations about what God is doing in their lives and in their neighborhoods. By creating spaces for mutual hospitality to occur, where meals can be shared in homes, cultural narratives shared, and stories told, leaders can shape environments where relationships characterized by mutuality and trust can begin to be formed.[47] As this happens, discomfort can be pressed into in ways that boundaries that were formerly static can be crossed. As they do this, God's everyday people in the Lighthouse may begin to experience true Gospel *shalom* in

---

46. Roxburgh and Romanuk, *Missional Leader*.
47. Branson and Martinez, *Churches, Cultures, and Leadership*, 240.

ways that God's manifold wisdom might be made known throughout the community (Eph 3:10–11).

SHAPING ENVIRONMENTS THROUGH PLURAL LEADERSHIP AT THE LIGHTHOUSE

Mark Branson suggests that local congregations participate in God's mission most effectively when a plurality of leaders shape environments where God's people can discern together how God might be inviting them to participate in his initiatives among them.[48] Based on her work in Acts, Adelina Alexe agrees with this perspective. Regarding Acts 15 specifically, she observes that the elders and apostles cultivated an environment characterized by collaboration, mutual submission, and respect, where the gathered people of God listened to one another and submitted to the guidance of the Holy Spirit (Acts 15:28) before discerning God's larger missional agenda among the Gentiles together. She sees this as part of a larger paradigm shift throughout Acts, suggesting that leadership roles often interweave for the good of the community.[49]

This approach presents a striking contrast with modern conceptions of ecclesial leadership, which tend to be characterized by hierarchy and direction more so than plurality and participation. Instead of a focus only on interior church life, there needs to be a dual focus that also seeks to connect churches more intimately to their contexts.[50] This is an important distinction because the task of leadership, then, becomes about shaping environments—or construction sites—where a community of interpreters can discern God's missional imagination for those people and join him in his work.[51] This requires a different skill-set than many leaders have been trained in today. Instead of providing answers and direction or monopolizing theological discourse as the experts, for example, they need to create spaces characterized by listening and dialogue, by theological reflection, and by reflection on encounters and experiences in the world.[52] They should seek to facilitate collaboration and partnership within the body of Christ—to create spaces where the various gifts of the Spirit, distributed to members of the body as the Spirit wills for the good of the body, can work

---

48. Branson, "Ecclesiology and Leadership," 41.
49. Alexe, "Acts of the Apostles," 179–80.
50. Branson, "Perspectives," 41–42.
51. Branson and Martinez, *Churches, Cultures, and Leadership*.
52. Van Gelder and Zscheile, *Missional Church*, 156.

together in mutuality and vulnerability—not just for the good of the body but also for the good of the world.[53]

What should be apparent by now is that leadership at The Lighthouse operates in a way that pushes against placing a priority on plural leadership that shapes environments. While not at all authoritarian, the model of charismatic leadership currently employed by Pastor Steve and many of the pastoral staff is not about shaping environments conducive to missional discernment and innovation among the everyday people of God. Instead, it is primarily about distribution—providing religious goods and services through high quality programs that will meet the needs of its religious constituents.

Charismatic Leadership as Distribution

This idea of leadership as distribution appears to characterize the unstated goal of leadership at The Lighthouse. The goal is to distribute as many high-quality programs as possible that will meet people's needs and introduce them to the life-saving Gospel of Jesus Christ. It is clear that while The Lighthouse's ecclesiology says that they believe in the giftedness and empowerment of the laity and that the Spirit is working in all, the real outworking of their approach says that innovation occurs top down. Missional initiatives for the most part are discerned at the top of the leadership hierarchy, implemented by the paid professionals, and provided for congregants and their neighbors. Congregants tend to be invited into the process to serve, and often to lead, but usually after the fact. What this means practically, then, is that gifted members are there to serve in ministries and programs dreamed up and initiated by the paid professionals rather than to participate in dreaming up and initiating them themselves. Many times, when lay leaders were invited in at the beginning of the process, the paid professionals unintentionally marginalized their voices or discounted them all together, as in the case of the drop-in center and computer training program in the community center.

What this serves to highlight, once again, is the clergy-centered leadership schema that continues to shape the life and mission praxis of the church. The philosophy and practice of leadership within the church reveals a clear hierarchy that begins with Pastor Steve, flows down through the staff, and ultimately reaches the people of God. This hierarchy serves to

---

53. Zscheile, "Trinity," 55–57.

thwart innovation on the margins through the ethnically diverse, everyday people of God, reinforces the church's mission-actional approach, and prevents the church from moving toward a more missional praxis as it seeks to participate in God's initiatives in the community.

The Potential of Interpretive Leadership at The Lighthouse

The clear implication of this discussion is that the top-down charismatic model of leadership that has built up and sustained The Lighthouse through the process of mission-actional change may hold it back now if leadership does not adapt. A charismatic leadership model, which is well suited for an attractional model of ministry, has difficulty keeping up with the trajectory toward missional because it is geared toward carrying out the vision of the leader rather than facilitating missional innovation among the people. The result of this top-down, staff-driven approach, however, is that there may be a great deal of untapped missional potential in the congregation. Consider, for example, that over 44 percent of the survey respondents indicated that they have an idea for reaching or serving people in the community that church leadership should know about. Even more telling, however, is that less than 13 percent of respondents said they did not, while over 42 percent were neutral on the subject. Due to the structure of the question and available responses, there are three likely possibilities for why respondents would have selected "neutral" on this question. It may indicate that many who answered "neutral" actually have an idea for outreach but are waiting for someone in leadership to approach them. It may mean that the respondents simply lack confidence in the quality of their idea and feel like it is not worth bringing to leadership. Or it could mean that they have already shared their idea with leadership and do not have anything new to add. Even without further clarification regarding these answers, the data indicates that there is likely a great deal of latent creativity and potential for missional innovation among congregants at The Lighthouse.

What this indicates is that the diverse members and regular attendees of the congregation who are not yet involved in ministry are an untapped resource for missional innovation. If pastoral leadership can learn how to tap into these resources by creating environments where congregational dialogue and discernment can occur, then the ideas that congregants currently have can be explored, examined, and refined through dialogue and listening. Then the creative potential of God's everyday people at The

Missiological Implications of the Leadership Praxis at The Lighthouse

Lighthouse can be unleashed, and the church may be able to move beyond its current ecclesio-centric, mission-actional praxis toward a more missional posture in its community. This, then, begs the question—how might leaders unleash the creative, missional potential of God's diverse people in other multiethnic congregations?

CULTIVATING MISSIONAL IDENTITY FORMATION IN MULTIETHNIC CHURCHES

Up to this point, I have presented a picture of the current mission praxis at The Lighthouse and how that praxis has been formed, over time, by the charismatic leadership approach employed by Pastor Steve and the pastoral staff. I have also reflected on how they might need to shift their leadership approach to shape a mission praxis that more faithfully embodies gospel life and mission in their community. Because the charismatic leadership approach employed at The Lighthouse is not uncommon among those leading multiethnic congregations in the North American mission context, however, the same shift is likely necessary in other situations as well.

According to Craig Van Gelder, every local church, as a community created by the Holy Spirit, "has a unique nature, or essence, which gives it a unique identity."[54] Accordingly, the way local churches respond to God's initiatives in their midst reveals who they understand themselves to be. In other words, "The church is. The church does what it is. The church organizes what it does."[55] It is important to note, however, that this is not a linear process that ends with theory applied to practice. If a church is engaging in ongoing interpretive work and reflection in construction sites, then these meanings and practices should continue to be formed and reformed over time in response to the way the Triune God is at work among them and in their changing context. In other words, the church should engage in praxis in a way that continues to shape her identity as a called and gathered people, sent by the Spirit into the world to participate in God's mission.

The nature of the discussion in this book has, I believe, clearly demonstrated this understanding of church life and mission. It has also shown the importance of plural leadership shaping environments—construction sites—where the process of missional identity formation can occur in multiethnic congregations. At The Lighthouse, the current mission-actional

---

54. Van Gelder, *Ministry*, 17.
55. Van Gelder, *Ministry*, 17.

praxis flows directly from diverse leaders' and congregants' perceptions of who they are as a church and how they should participate in God's initiatives in their context. Because their self-perception is highly ecclesio-centric, the missional initiatives in their community tend to be less about discerning and participating with God's initiatives as they are about initiating activities that will build up the church and transform the community. The diverse perspectives brought by the ethnically diverse, everyday people of God are rarely, if ever, factored into the discernment process, and because of this, there is likely a great deal of untapped missional potential lying dormant within the congregation.

The approach to missional leadership that I develop in this section presents a unique understanding of how leaders of multiethnic congregations can form a missional identity, or DNA, that will shape their gospel life and mission together. I draw on Roxburgh's model of leaders cultivating a new core identity for churches in a changed environment,[56] Van Gelder's four-dimension approach to spiritual discernment,[57] and Branson's leadership triad as he and Martinez apply it in multiethnic congregational environments.[58]

The Multiethnic Church in Relationship to Its Context

Alan Roxburgh has done extensive work explaining the current sociocultural context characterized by discontinuous change in the North American mission context.[59] As a result of this work, he suggests that a church's relationship to its context needs to change. Drawing on the work of Paul Hiebert,[60] he suggests that churches can no longer view themselves as bounded sets, closed off to those who operate outside of their traditions and commitments. Instead, they need to view themselves as centered sets, with much less rigid boundaries determining who is in and who is out so that the distinctions between "us and them" can begin to be broken down.[61] This posture shift, represented by a dotted boundary line in the image

---

56. Roxburgh, *Missional Map-Making*, 136–88.
57. Van Gelder, *Ministry*, 115.
58. Branson and Martinez, *Churches, Cultures, and Leadership*, 212–26.
59. See Roxburgh and Romanuk, *Missional Leader*; Roxburgh, *Missional Map-Making*; *Missional*.
60. Hiebert, *Missiological Implications*.
61. Roxburgh, *Missional Map-Making*, 135.

Missiological Implications of the Leadership Praxis at The Lighthouse

below,⁶² allows the diverse people of God in local congregations to relate to their neighbors as subjects and active participants in God's redemptive initiatives rather than as objects of mission. It presents new opportunities for leaders and congregants alike to form the relationships necessary to gain new insights into what God is already doing in the lives of their neighbors and in their communities.

Shaping Environments Among the Diverse People of God

According to Roxburgh, the work of leadership in this type of congregational atmosphere is about cultivating environments where the everyday people of God can learn and engage in new practices that will expand their missional imagination.⁶³ Practices such as personal and corporate listening and discernment, personal and group listening to the Holy Spirit's promptings in scripture, and mutual hospitality can be especially helpful

---

62. See Figure 15.
63. Roxburgh, *Missional Map-Making*, 139.

Charismatic Leadership and Missional Change

here as the everyday people of God re-learn what it means to re-connect with God and their neighbors on the ground.[64] As I discussed earlier, leaders need to provide space for these corporate practices to occur in formal and informal construction sites for meaningful interpretive work to occur, represented by the various circles on and within the permeable boundary between church and community in the following image.

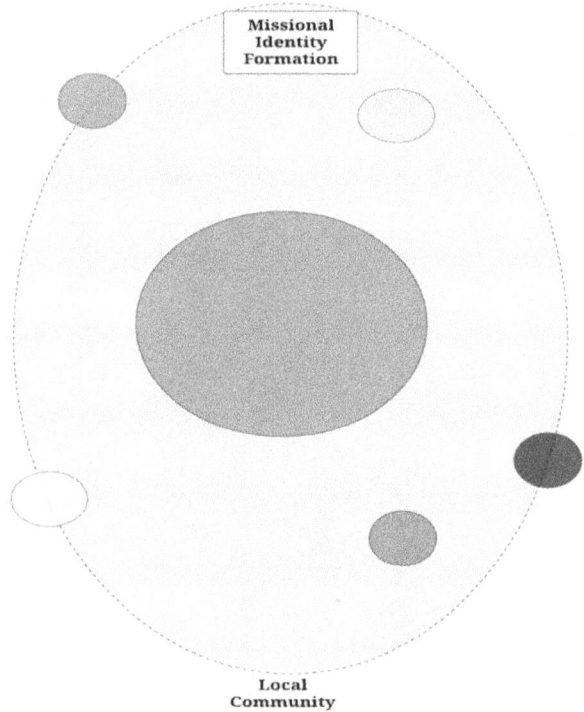

Each of these circles represents the different environments where the diverse people of God are coming together to share gospel life among themselves and with their neighbors—treating them as subject/agents in God's initiatives rather than as objects—to discern through their corporate practices where God might be calling them to join in his ongoing redemptive work. The different colors, sizes, and locations of these circles represent the priority of the diverse people of God coming together across boundaries—racial, ethnic, cultural, gender, socio-economic, and spiritual—in different ways. The nature of these diverse groups is determined by the unique

64. Roxburgh, *Missional Map-Making*, 147–61.

make-up of different churches in different communities. It is important to note here that the circles on the boundary of church/community represent the need for these practices to occur with and among neighbors, not just within the friendly confines of the church. This helps discernment to occur among the ethnically diverse, everyday people of God on the margins of church life, not just among the centers of power.

Conceiving of the process this way reflects the connectedness of the first two elements of Branson's leadership triad, interpretive and relational leadership. Gathering the ethnically diverse people of God into construction sites represents leaders forming an interpretive community to shape new meanings and practices together. It also demonstrates the necessity of weaving new relational networks across boundaries that formerly divided to nourish "church participants and neighbors toward love and synergism."[65] In multiethnic congregations, plural leaders shaping these diverse relational networks helps to ensure that voices from below are protected and that participants can discern what God is doing on the margins of church life, where real relationships between church participants and neighbors are nurtured. It is only then that the resulting practices, experiments, and new forms of gospel life that characterize his third element, implemental leadership, can be discerned and implemented.

Discerning God's Initiatives in Multiethnic Congregations

Before engaging in new forms of gospel life and mission together, it is important for leaders, diverse church participants, and neighbors to engage in the type of interpretive work necessary to accurately discern what God is up to in a given context. In diverse communities, God is at work in many different ways. The ways that particular congregations join him in that work will depend on how the unique nature of that church—including the unique gifts and strengths, passions, experiences, theological traditions, and understandings—all intersect with the opportunities within their communities where the Spirit is inviting them to join. According to Van Gelder, this requires interpretive work to be carried out in any of the construction sites established by leaders in four interpretive dimensions—texts, context, church (community), and strategy (experiments, initiatives, new practices).[66]

---

65. Branson and Martinez, *Churches, Cultures, and Leadership*, 213.
66. Van Gelder, *Ministry*.

Charismatic Leadership and Missional Change

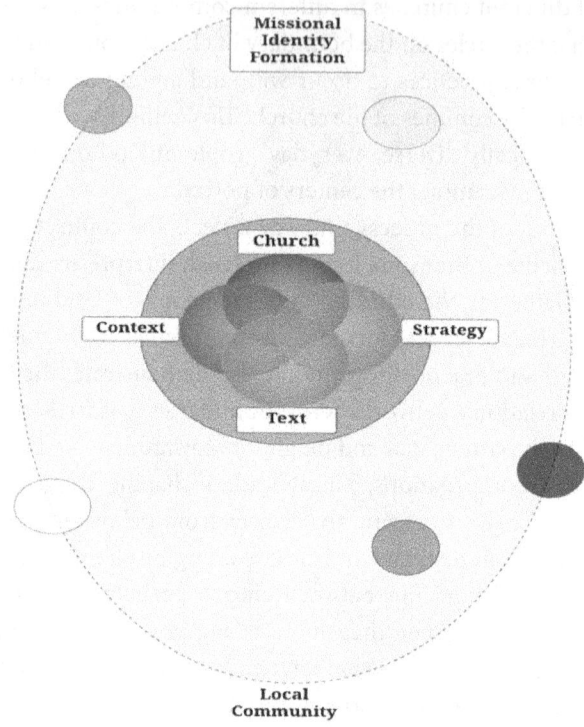

The interpretive work carried out by ethnically diverse leaders, participants, and neighbors in these relational networks is not a one-time experience. Rather, it is an ongoing process of discernment that engages the church in praxis. Through praxis, that ongoing cycle of action/engagement and study/reflection, church leaders and participants continually interpret their ongoing participation with God's initiatives in light of the new meanings emerging from their new reality.[67] This focuses the church on discerning the way God's initiatives on the ground may be changing over time as the context and the church changes.

Discerning Adaptive Challenges in Multiethnic Congregations

Engaging in interpretive work in construction sites also helps leaders and church participants to identify any values, assumptions, and practices that may be hindering their ability to form a new missional identity. As I have already discussed extensively, multiethnic congregations—especially

---

67. Branson and Martinez, *Churches, Cultures, and Leadership*, 37–49.

those led by charismatic leaders—face particular adaptive challenges requiring new learning if they are to shed ecclesio-centric forms of mission and embody a more faithful form of gospel life in their communities. The process of identifying and addressing these adaptive challenges lies at the heart of missional identity construction and requires deeper reflective and analytical work by the entire people of God. Leaders and congregants need to reflect on the cultural and theological schemas that are informing their current understandings, values, and assumptions about the nature of leadership and gospel life, God, and his initiatives in their context.

The diagram below reflects how these forces shape the nature of the interpretive work that needs to occur in multiethnic congregations. It is crucial for leaders and church participants alike to identify which cultural schemas are impinging upon them and how those schemas differ among ethnically diverse church leaders and participants. They can then better understand the different ways that people from each group understand the nature of leadership, gospel life together, and God's initiatives in their midst. It is also important that they understand how their existing and forming theological understandings are both shaping and being shaped by the cultural schemas at work in their midst. Without these understandings, they will be unable to recognize and address the sociocultural forces that are shaping the adaptive challenges they are facing.

Charismatic Leadership and Missional Change

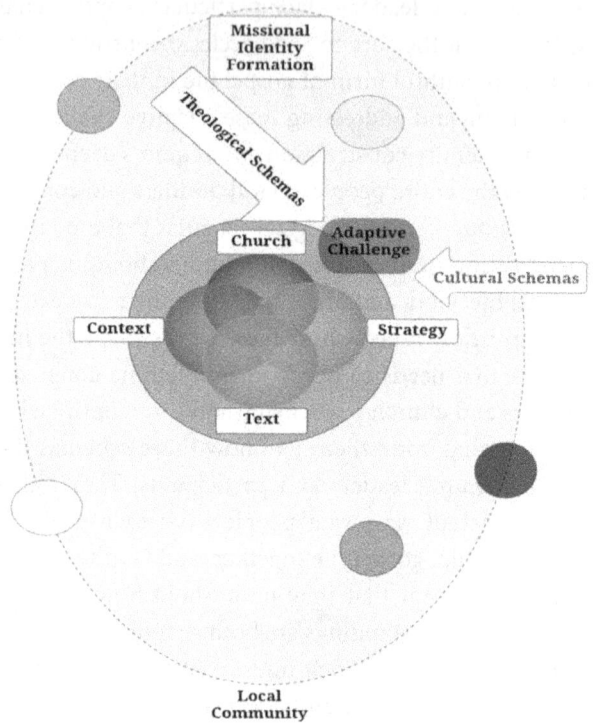

Participating in God's Initiatives as a Multiethnic Church

As church leaders and participants identify and address the adaptive challenges they are facing, they can more accurately discern and join God in his initiatives in their communities. As they allow their ongoing interpretive work, their engagement with the gospel narratives, and their experiences with their neighbors to reshape their values, assumptions, and beliefs, they can discern where God might be inviting them to join him in exciting new partnerships and initiatives with their neighbors and their communities.[68] The nature of these partnerships and other initiatives will be determined by how who they are—the unique gifts, strengths, passions, experiences, and resources they possess—intersects with what God is doing in the lives of their neighbors and communities. As they respond to God's invitation, they can then more faithfully participate in

68. Roxburgh, *Missional Map-Making*, 163–88.

new forms of gospel life and mission together with God and with their neighbors. This enables them to live more faithfully into their forming identity as a missional people who have been called, gathered, and sent by God into the particular communities where they reside.

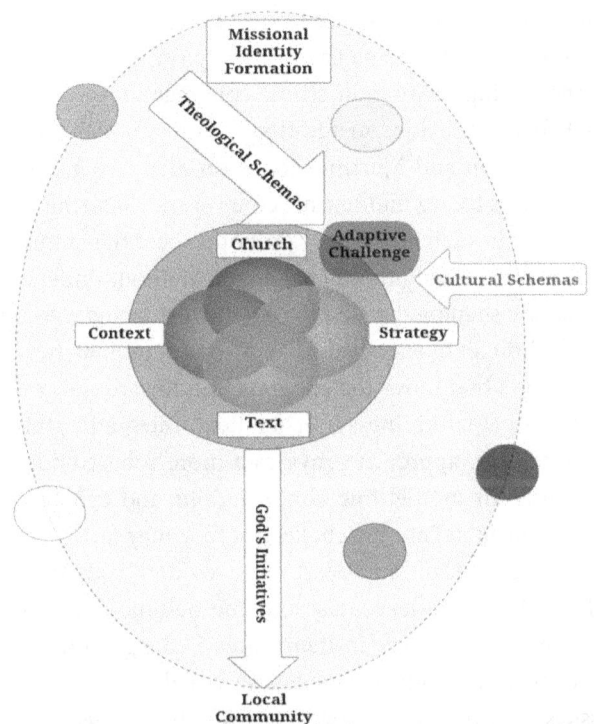

BRIDGING THE MISSIONAL LEADERSHIP AND MULTIETHNIC CHURCH CONVERSATIONS

As should be clear from the preceding discussion, the approach I am proposing bridges the missional leadership and multiethnic congregation conversations in ways that are similar to Branson and Martinez. It is a praxis-based model that draws on Heifetz and Linsky's adaptive leadership framework to explain the nature and process of missional change in multiethnic congregations. It goes beyond Branson and Martinez's work in three significant ways, however. First, by substituting the concept of construction sites for Heifetz and Linsky's understanding of holding environments, I have reframed the understanding of what occurs in these sites. Identifying and addressing the adaptive challenges that are inhibiting congregational life and mission is actually a process of missional identity formation among the people of God. This process is iterative and occurs over time resulting in new praxis—a new way of understanding and participating in the *missio Dei* as a multiethnic community of believers.

Second, my use of schema theory to explore the nature of the adaptive challenges facing many multiethnic congregations as they participate in missional change provides an additional level of understanding into the issue. While Branson and Martinez focus on identifying, and addressing adaptive challenges facing multiethnic congregations during the process of missional change in their work, they do not discuss the cultural and theological schemas underlying those challenges. Without understanding how these schemas are shaping the adaptive challenges facing the congregation, it is extremely difficult to effectively diagnose and, ultimately, address these challenges in ways that move the congregation toward new expressions of mission and Gospel faithfulness in its context. Integrating this theoretical framework into their approach provides a more robust understanding of missional change in multiethnic congregations and can provide leaders with additional insights into the challenges they may face.

Third, while Branson and Martinez provide a composite case study compiled from their experience in several multiethnic churches as they discuss leading missional change in their book, I engage in thick description through a detailed case study that depicts an actual situation with real people and real issues. Through this research, I have brought missional and multiethnic theoretical frameworks together through empirical research, which allows me to make a theoretical contribution that has not been presented in the context of live church situations before—the "Mission-actional" church. Rather than a more theoretical view, drawing on many possible situations, then, I provide original research that demonstrates how incorporating these theoretical frameworks might benefit those leading missional change at The Lighthouse. The result is a rich case study that can inform missional leadership praxis and contribute toward an important and burgeoning scholarly discussion, as I will discuss in my Conclusion.

SUMMARY

In this chapter I have reflected on the current leadership praxis at The Lighthouse through the lenses of four missional priorities in light of two key Lukan narratives. I have demonstrated that, for the most part, the church is not currently living into these priorities because of the top-down charismatic approach to leadership that is contributing toward an ecclesiocentric mission praxis. This mission praxis is largely pastor-driven, devoid of meaningful relationships with neighbors in the community, and focused on providing religious goods and services for the community. It has also suppressed missional innovation and creativity among the ethnically diverse people of God and limited the church's ability to interpret and respond to the Spirit's initiatives in its context. Instead, mission events and programs tend to be initiated by the church through leadership, devoid of true collaboration and partnership with their neighbors. This has prevented the church from living into a truly missional posture and has it instead engaging its community through a mission-actional approach focused on activities and events in and for the community.

I have also presented a unique leadership model that provides an alternative understanding of missional identity formation for The Lighthouse and other multiethnic congregations. I have demonstrated that by utilizing the theoretical frameworks I have applied to my data, leaders of local multiethnic congregations can more effectively discern and participate in God's redemptive initiatives in their midst and among their neighbors. As plural leaders protect voices from below by establishing construction sites where interpretive work and discernment can occur, diverse church leaders and participants alike can form the types of meaningful subject-subject relationships with their neighbors that are necessary to discern God's work on the ground. They can begin to weave the type of diverse relational networks that are necessary for the church to more faithfully embody Gospel life and mission across boundaries that formerly divided. In doing so, they can glorify God and make his manifold wisdom known in their communities and beyond (Eph 3:10).

6

Making the Case for Interpretive Leadership at The Lighthouse

ONE OF MY GOALS when I began this book was to share findings from research conducted at The Lighthouse that might challenge current conceptions of top-down leadership and transform the way pastors facilitate missional change in multiethnic congregations. To achieve this goal, I explored how the pastoral leadership approach at The Lighthouse engages ethnically diverse congregants in the process of missional change by answering four research questions: (1) What is the nature of missional change occurring at The Lighthouse? (2) Why have pastors led missional change the way they have at The Lighthouse? (3) What is the nature of ethnic diversity present at The Lighthouse? (4) How has pastoral leadership fostered or impeded ethnically diverse congregants' involvement in the process? In this chapter, I will present several conclusions in response to those questions. Together, they make a case for the value of interpretive leadership at The Lighthouse and, ultimately, for other multiethnic congregations seeking to transition into missional ministry as well.

MISSION-ACTIONAL MINISTRY AT THE LIGHTHOUSE

In response to my first research question—what is the nature of missional change occurring at The Lighthouse—I suggest that the process of missional change engaged in by members of The Lighthouse community is actually not a journey toward missional at all. In light of their current approach to leadership, the church's current mission praxis—one I have described as mission-actional—is likely it's final destination. The priorities of The Lighthouse leadership are still heavily centered on what happens on Sunday—on getting people through the doors to worship and, ultimately, plugged into a ministry that will meet their spiritual growth needs. In other words, while The Lighthouse has significantly increased its mission activities in its community and beyond over the years, its mission praxis is still heavily ecclesio-centric. As such, The Lighthouse fits squarely into what Van Gelder and Zscheile identify as the first branch—Discovering—and first sub-branch—Missional as Missions and Great Commission Obedience—on their "Missional Family Tree."[1] Churches that fall into this category tend to place a heavy emphasis on human agency in their mission praxis, as being missional is seen primarily as people and churches responding obediently to the Great Commission. The emphasis is placed not so much on discerning God's initiatives in a given context as it is on engaging that context in response to a leader's vision and resulting strategy.

This description seems to fit the current mission praxis and philosophy of leadership practiced at The Lighthouse quite well. As I have demonstrated throughout this book, the top-down, charismatic approach to leadership at The Lighthouse relies heavily on Pastor's Steve's ability to discern and cast vision to the church. It also relies heavily on his ability to motivate through his charisma and spiritual authority and to innovate out of his—as well as his paid professional staff's—giftedness and expertise. As he has invited the congregation to focus more and more on engaging the "one-mile radius" that comprises their immediate community, he has done so primarily emphasizing God's desire to transform the community through obedience to the Great Commission and loving and serving their diverse neighbors. This has translated into an approach that focuses not so much on discerning God's initiatives in their community but rather on initiating ministries and events they believe will impact the community, like the community center, Church Without Walls, and Serve Day.

While this approach has undoubtedly produced some fruitful results, it also carries with it some underlying theological and ecclesiological deficiencies that inform the church's mission praxis. For example, in emphasizing their own agency in missional discernment, decision-making, and implementation processes, leadership is unwittingly minimizing the Spirit's agency in the process. While they still seek God's direction through

---

1. Van Gelder and Zscheile, *Missional Church*, 68.

prayer, scripture, and occasional conversation with informants, there is little emphasis placed on discerning the Spirit's ongoing activities in their context. This has ultimately served to minimize the role of the Spirit in their mission praxis and has contributed toward a cycle that reinforces the top-down, charismatic leadership approach. This, in turn, has served to diminish agency among the everyday people of God, as it centers power among the paid professionals. Thus, while church leadership has an ecclesiology that says they value the giftedness and contributions of the everyday people of God, functionally, they engage in practices that diminish the role of people in the congregation. This ultimately reinforces the clergy-centered ministry schema that continues to shape congregational life and ministry in the church and subtly communicates to members that they are only suited for certain tasks. The truly important work, on the other hand, is best left to the paid professionals. This serves to strengthen an adaptive challenge that I discussed in chapter 4—the congregation's over-dependence on the charismatic leader.

FOLLOWING EXISTING MAPS TO MISSION-ACTIONAL

In response to my second research question—why have pastors led missional change the way they have at The Lighthouse—I suggest that Pastor Steve and other pastoral leaders have been following the wrong maps. Using the metaphor of map-making, Roxburgh suggests that the challenge facing many pastoral leaders today is that they are following outdated maps shaped by modernity. These maps—what I have been referring to as leadership schemas—are about control, clarity, and certainty.[2] In church settings, they reinforce reliance on proven techniques and methods of church growth, performance metrics, and the training, knowledge, and skills of the paid professional. However, these maps, shaped by modernity, do not provide accurate directions in today's constantly shifting sociocultural context characterized by discontinuous change—they no longer describe the reality we find ourselves in. They depend on predictability and control, whereas the current context is characterized by "disequilibrium, anxiety, confusion, and disorientation."[3] Because of this, leaders in the church need new maps,

---

2. Roxburgh, *Missional Map-Making*, 24.
3. Roxburgh, *Missional Map-Making*, 16.

but more than this, they need to be missional map-makers "that re-create a core identity among the people of a local church."[4]

Roxburgh's metaphor is helpful, as it highlights salient themes in my findings relating to the cultural schemas that are shaping the leadership praxis at The Lighthouse. I have discussed at length how the top-down, charismatic leadership schema employed by Pastor Steve and other pastors in the church has reinforced a cycle of over-dependence on the charismatic leader. I have also analyzed how this adaptive challenge has been reinforced by the clergy-centered ministry schema shaping both the clergy's and congregation's missional imagination and the consumerist values that shape so many of the congregants who come to the church as religious consumers. The combination of these cultural factors has caused Pastor Steve and the leadership to operate out of the cultural map they know best—pastor as expert. Following this map has caused Pastor Steve and other pastors to initiate and drive the change process and to center discernment and decision-making for new mission initiatives with them. This has marginalized the voices of the vast majority of congregants in the process, especially people of color.

This map-making metaphor further explains how the church has arrived at its current mission-actional praxis. The books that have reshaped Pastor Steve and Ella's missional imagination[5] have not created new maps suited to the church's ethnically dynamic and culturally shifting context. Instead, they have created a new map that maximizes Pastor Steve's strengths as a charismatic and visionary leader and fit his missiological schemas of obedience to the Great Commandment, event over process, and church growth. For Pastor Steve, then, this ecclesio-centric, mission-actional map seems to be the church's best pathway forward because it may provide a level of control and familiarity in the midst of uncertainty and change.

A resulting problem from this ecclesio-centric, mission-actional map, however, is that in spite of their desire to reconnect with and impact their immediate community, the church actually remains disconnected from their context in some significant ways. In essence, many in leadership and the congregation are treating their community as a geographic container full of mission targets rather than as their "place," characterized by relationship, shared memory, and lived experience with their neighbors.[6] This has

---

4. Roxburgh, *Missional Map-Making*, 134.
5. See especially Rusaw and Swanson, *Externally Focused*.
6. See Inge, *Christian Theology of Place*.

contributed toward paternalistic forms of ministry, centering on events and projects among their neighbors rather than expressions of ministry based in deep and meaningful relationships with their neighbors. Because of this, many in leadership and the congregation remain relatively blind to the ways that systems resulting from racialization and injustice continue to shape the daily experiences of their ethnically diverse neighbors as well as their own congregational life and mission praxis. Thus, in spite of their stated value for carrying out God's mission in their local community as a multiethnic, reconciled community of believers, they largely fail to consistently live out this value in a way that truly accounts for their context.

HINDERING MISSIONAL INNOVATION AND CREATIVITY AMONG ETHNICALLY DIVERSE CONGREGANTS

In response to my third and fourth research questions—what is the nature of ethnic diversity present at The Lighthouse, and how has pastoral leadership fostered or impeded diverse congregants' involvement in the process—I suggest that as a resource for change, charismatic leadership has hindered innovation and creativity among ethnically diverse congregants in the process of missional change at The Lighthouse. On the one hand, Pastor Steve has used this resource—in conjunction with the missional theology of place that he has been constructing within the congregation—to drive a great deal of mission-actional change in the church. On the other hand, his top-down, charismatic approach is working to suppress missional innovation and creativity among the ethnically diverse, everyday people of God in the congregation.

According to Branson and Martinez, a central task of leadership in multiethnic congregations is shaping environments where the entire church, and the various "groups of people within the church, are learning how to discern the initiatives of the Holy Spirit in their midst and in their neighborhoods and are developing experiments and practices that increase everyone's participation in God's grace."[7] Zscheile concurs, suggesting that it is in these environments that God's people can reflect on how the Spirit is at work in their lives and in the lives of their neighbors so that their missional imagination can be stirred and innovation and creativity released.[8] This requires leaders to protect leadership voices from below so that the diverse gifts and

---

7. Branson and Martinez, *Churches, Cultures, and Leadership*, 225.
8. Zscheile, *Agile Church*, 89–92.

perceptions, values, and views of all are heard, and the missional imagination of the entire people of God can be stirred "by God's initiatives for them and their neighbors."[9] Unfortunately, these leadership voices from below are usually not protected at The Lighthouse, and the environments necessary to give them a place in the process are largely absent. The current approach at The Lighthouse has been to place discernment and decision-making processes at the center of power among the paid staff. Instead of stirring missional imagination, then, this has served to marginalize voices that could be most helpful in the discernment process—the ethnically diverse, everyday people of God who live with and among their neighbors.

This issue is exacerbated when we consider the importance of discovering open spaces where learning conversations can occur with the church's neighbors.[10] Because the Euro-centric leadership schema that is shaping leadership selection processes has contributed toward an ethnic hierarchy in the church, congregants of color have been disproportionately marginalized in The Lighthouse's mission praxis. This means that those who are most vitally connected to the church's neighbors are rarely—if ever—invited into the discernment process. This potentially disconnects those with the most to offer from the discernment and decision-making process and significantly limits the missional imagination of the congregation.[11]

As I consider this issue, it places the church in a conundrum. On the one hand, Pastor Steve's top-down, charismatic approach has led the church to unprecedented growth, new expressions of mission activities in their community and beyond, and a level of ethnic diversity that is highly congruent with their community. His charismatic style has served the church well, and he has not used his influence in ways that are considered abusive or inappropriate. To the contrary, he is a loved and highly respected pastoral leader by the overwhelming majority of the congregation and ministry staff. The level of satisfaction with the vision and direction of the church, in spite of some of the complaints with his decision-making style, is exceptionally high, and people seem to be overwhelmingly on board with where he is leading the church.

On the other hand, Pastor Steve's leadership style fights against the very direction that he is trying to move the church. By centering power and decision-making for missional innovation around himself and the

---

9. Branson and Martinez, *Churches, Cultures, and Leadership*, 224–31.
10. Zscheile, *Agile Church*, 98.
11. Van Gelder and Zscheile, *Missional Church*.

predominantly Caucasian decision-makers, he has limited the church's ability to engage in small, iterative experiments born out of close listening relationships with ethnically diverse neighbors that are so essential to facilitating innovation.[12] By keeping their ethnically diverse congregants on the margins of discernment and decision-making, and by leading and initiating new ministries from the center, he reinforces the clergy-centered ministry schema that puts more of the burden for ministry on the paid professionals. This serves to reinforce a point I highlighted in chapter 4—while a charismatic approach is well suited to an attractional model of ministry, it is less suited for a missional approach because it centers power, decision-making, and influence with the heroic leader. In the case of The Lighthouse, it also de-centers power and decision-making from the ethnically diverse people of God who could potentially expand the missional imagination of the congregation.

RELEASING MISSIONAL POTENTIAL AT THE LIGHTHOUSE THROUGH INTERPRETIVE LEADERSHIP

In light of these conclusions, I suggest that a shift in Pastor Steve's leadership style is required to shape a new missional identity at the Lighthouse—one where the ethnically diverse, everyday people of God can have their missional imagination shaped by God's initiatives in their midst. Indeed, a shift seems to be required even to sustain the current mission-actional praxis, as I previously discussed. I demonstrated that there is a significant gap between a lived and preferred value for missional among the congregation. This gap is largely due to the clergy-centered ministry schema that is embedded within the congregation, and that is reinforced by the top-down, charismatic leadership approach employed by Pastor Steve and the staff. Because of this, the gap is unlikely to improve significantly under the current leadership approach. Without getting the congregation more involved in discerning and decision-making processes where they can engage in storytelling and listen to what the Spirit is doing in their lives and the lives of their neighbors, they are unlikely to find new motivation to get involved in outreach focused ministries. Instead, many are likely to remain religious consumers, looking to have their religious, social, and emotional needs met through programs in the church.

---

12. Zscheile, *Agile Church*, 65–67.

There is an upside to this dilemma, however. As I have discussed, there is a great deal of untapped missional potential lying dormant within the congregation. While the existing leadership approach is unlikely to tap into this potential in a meaningful way, a shift in the current philosophy may yield significant results. The charismatic qualities characteristic of Pastor Steve's leadership that have driven change to its current point can also be a significant resource moving forward. The issue that Pastor Steve needs to consider is whether he is willing to channel his charismatic qualities in new ways. He needs to decide whether he will work to reframe the ecclesio-centric form of mission the church is currently engaged in by shaping the environments necessary to cultivate a new missional imagination among the everyday people of God.[13] By providing construction sites that invite voices from the margins of church life to participate with the centers of power, existing assumptions, values, perceptions, practices, and challenges can be named and ultimately reframed through generative dialogue, scripture meditation, cultural analysis, reflection, and prayer. As this occurs, leaders and congregants alike can begin to live into a new missional identity.

---

13. Branson and Martinez, *Churches, Cultures, and Leadership*, 231.

Conclusion

IF THERE IS ONE thing that research has revealed over the last several years, it is that leading missional change in local congregations is a challenging process. What I have demonstrated in this book is that leading missional change in multiethnic congregations can be even more challenging, especially when relying on the top-down, charismatic, ecclesio-centric forms of leadership so popular among many pastors today. I have challenged these conceptions of top-down leadership through my research at The Lighthouse, and I have instead proposed interpretive leadership as a pathway forward for those seeking to lead missional change in multiethnic congregations. Doing so, I suggest, will help those leading multiethnic congregations more effectively liberate and utilize the collective gifts and wisdom of their diverse membership as they continue to reshape their mission praxis in biblically faithful and contextually appropriate ways. As I conclude this conversation, I briefly offer three implications of my research for pastoral leaders at The Lighthouse, for those leading other multiethnic congregations, and for those seeking to conduct further research at the intersection of multiethnic ministry and missional change.

IMPLICATIONS FOR MISSIONAL LEADERSHIP AT THE LIGHTHOUSE

Throughout this book, I have made a case for the value of interpretive leadership as a means of releasing the untapped missional potential of diverse congregants at The Lighthouse. Accordingly, if Pastor Steve can use his influence to shape construction sites where congregational dialogue and discernment can occur, he can begin to reshape the mission praxis of the congregation in ways that are generative and that inspire creativity among the everyday people of God. Ethnically diverse and marginalized voices—from both inside and outside of the congregation—can come together to share where they sense God actively working in their lives. Together, congregants and leaders can listen, learn, and dream about the initiatives God may be inviting them to join. Ideas can be explored and ultimately implemented through small iterative experiments as the missional imagination of the congregation grows.[1] In this way, Pastor Steve can begin to give the work of ministry back to the people. This can yield greater levels of missional innovation and creativity among the ethnically diverse congregants at the Lighthouse as well as an increased capacity to address the adaptive challenges facing the congregation as the church continues to move into its neighborhood. It may also shift the church's journey further, toward a more missional posture that embraces their identity as a called and gathered people, sent to participate with God in his initiatives, with, rather than to, their neighbors.

Author's like David P. Leong[2] and Mark Gornik[3] highlight the importance of this posture shift for leaders and congregants at The Lighthouse. As they focus less on events and projects and instead enter into deep and meaningful relationships with their neighbors, leaders and congregants alike can begin to truly embody a value for "place." They can create new sacred spaces through lived experience with their ethnically diverse neighbors that result in new shared memories together. They can begin a journey toward God's *shalom* that takes their context more seriously and that might reshape their own congregational life and mission praxis as a truly reconciled multiethnic community. As they do so, they might see God's Kingdom truly manifest in North Port City in ways that are unexpected, yet exactly what they hope for.

IMPLICATIONS FOR MISSIONAL LEADERSHIP IN MULTIETHNIC CONGREGATIONS

My findings, while specific to The Lighthouse, also carry implications for those attempting to lead missional change in other multiethnic congregations. As I previously discussed, the majority of current literature

---

1. Branson and Martinez, *Churches, Cultures, and Leadership*, 224–26.
2. See Leong, *Race and Place*.
3. See Gornik, *To Live in Peace*.

targeting churches emphasizes top-down, hierarchical approaches to change leadership that depend on the skills and abilities of a heroic leader. Agency is centered primarily in the leader, who is called to discern God's vision for the church, cast that vision to the congregation, and implement initiatives that will lead the church toward a bright new future. Due to the unique challenges associated with multiethnic ministry, literature in this field is especially prone to this understanding. A charismatic leader who can inspire people across ethnic boundaries and address any challenges encountered during the change process with their skills and expertise is particularly valued.

My research challenges these assumptions about leadership, however. While a charismatic, leader-centered approach can produce fruitful results in the process of missional change, it is ultimately limited in the types of results it can produce. By this, I do not mean numerical limits, or even Kingdom influence. The numerical growth, multiplication, and expanded regional and international influence through The Lighthouse are evidence of that. The results that can be produced in the everyday people of God in a given multiethnic congregation, however, are limited. As I have demonstrated, charismatic leadership carries with it inherent qualities that can result in adaptive challenges difficult for a multiethnic congregation to identify and address. Rather than serving as a counter-cultural model of racial reconciliation and social equality for marginalized voices, ethnic hierarchies can be perpetuated that mirror those in the American cultural context at large. Further, by centering power for discernment and decision-making in hierarchical leadership, the Spirit's agency is minimized, and the missional imagination of God's people is stifled as the environments necessary to stimulate that imagination are absent.

Contrasting this, my research suggests the value of leaders engaging the entire congregation in the process of missional change. If leaders of multiethnic churches can channel their influence in ways that nurture the missional imagination of God's people, they can increase their capacity for missional innovation and creativity. This ultimately strengthens the entire congregation because it gives the work of ministry back to those who are best positioned to discern the Spirit's initiatives on the margins of church life and in their respective communities—the ethnically diverse everyday people of God. One way leaders can accomplish this is by setting up construction sites where storytelling, listening to the Spirit of God, and discernment can occur among ethnically diverse church participants and leadership and, when possible, with their neighbors. As the Spirit's movements are discerned, small, iterative, missional experiments can be created and implemented. This ultimately places agency where it belongs—with the Spirit of God—and invites the entire congregation to discern and join in on His initiatives in their context rather than depending on the vision and giftedness of the leader. It can also help them to identify potential obstacles and even adaptive challenges that may hinder these experiments or other moves of God in their midst.

There are several methods pastoral leaders can utilize to accomplish this goal. Leaders can facilitate these environments within existing structures and programs such as small groups or Sunday school classes. Separate listening groups can be established throughout the congregation[4] or out in the neighborhood, in coffee shops or restaurants, where neighbors can also be engaged. Existing missional change methods, such as the Missional Change Model,[5] Appreciative Inquiry,[6] or other system-wide approaches can be utilized by leaders to stimulate the missional imagination of the congregation. The specific method, like other issues relating to leadership, will be best determined as local leaders discern the make-up and culture of their congregation and the unique context their church is situated in.

I realize, however, that for leaders who have been trained in current approaches to change leadership and are shaped by the top-down, charismatic leadership schema that is popular today, this will be a significant paradigm shift. For many, it will likely be an adaptive challenge that will not be easy for them to recognize, address, and ultimately overcome without assistance. For this reason, I recommend that leaders establish construction sites for themselves, where they can undergo their own process of personal change and identity formation. One example of this would be entering into a coaching relationship, where they can form the "lateral bonds of affection, trust, and camaraderie" necessary to identify and address the competing commitments and ultimate concerns informing the adaptive challenges they might be facing.[7] An even more effective approach would be entering into a peer mentoring or learning group with other pastors, facilitated by a coach, where they can explore these issues in the safety of relationships with those they can identify with. Whichever approach is chosen, the important

---

4. See Roxburgh and Romanuk, *Missional Leader*.
5. Roxburgh and Romanuk, *Missional Leader*.
6. Branson, *Memories, Hopes, and Conversations*.
7. Heifetz, Grashow, and Linsky, *Adaptive Leadership*, 156.

thing is for pastors to surround themselves with the support they need to begin, engage, and remain in the process for the duration.

As pastoral leaders in multiethnic congregations embrace this call to practice interpretive leadership, they accomplish some important goals. First, they give the Spirit of God priority in the change process, which places the leader and the congregation in a posture of responsiveness rather than of initiating. Second, they put ethnically diverse congregants in environments where the Spirit of God can stimulate their missional imagination, which allows the Spirit to work among and through the everyday people of God in new and exciting ways. Third, they invite formerly marginalized voices from below into the discernment process, which helps to eliminate ethnic hierarchies that may have formed within the congregation. Fourth, they strengthen their churches in ways that will help them last beyond their tenure as they break cycles of over-dependence on their leadership. While this work may be difficult, it is fruitful and necessary if multiethnic churches are to reach their full missional potential in the diverse communities where God has placed them.

IMPLICATIONS FOR FURTHER RESEARCH

Based on the nature of my findings, there are some implications for further research. First, while this research has provided valuable theoretical foundations upon which to develop missional leadership theory for those leading multiethnic congregations, findings from a single case study cannot be generalized to other churches due to the unique contextual factors at the research site. By conducting a collective case study, then, findings from other settings can be compared to formulate missional leadership theory that is generalizable to a broader spectrum of churches. Choosing a broad cross-section of multiethnic congregations of different sizes that are in different regions of the country; that are in different stages of their missional identity formation; and that are being led by leaders from different cultural backgrounds can account for variables that might be unique to one particular setting while identifying those that might be common to all. The result of this type of study, then, can be a more robust theory that can shape new missional praxis for leaders of multiethnic congregations in different environments.

Second, it is important to explore the usefulness of interpretive leadership as an approach for ministry leadership in multiethnic congregations. While my findings demonstrate the potential of interpretive leadership to facilitate missional innovation among the diverse people of God in multiethnic congregations, the best way to tangibly prove this is to test it through experimentation. One way to accomplish this is by implementing a system-wide action-research approach such as Appreciative Inquiry or the Missional Change Model in several multiethnic churches, which would allow for both practice and research to be conducted simultaneously. This would ultimately fortify the theory developed through the research conducted at The Lighthouse by providing observations of the approaches I am proposing here. It would also contribute toward a more robust theory of missional leadership in multiethnic congregations that is shaped through praxis.

CONCLUDING THOUGHTS

As I close this discussion, I would like to highlight the fact that The Lighthouse has come a long way on its journey. It has come as far as it has because God has blessed the church with a charismatic, visionary leader who saw potential where few others did. He has led the church with integrity and as faithfully and responsively to the Spirit as he knew how. He has utilized the resources at his disposal to the best of his ability, and the results have been beyond anything anyone could have anticipated. Under Pastor Steve's leadership, the church has grown and expanded its influence for Christ and his Kingdom far beyond the dreams that any of those one hundred members likely had when they called him to serve as their senior pastor more than two decades ago. Dozens of churches have been planted throughout the region and across the globe. The church has grown from one to three services every Sunday. Exciting ministries, including a new community center and partnership with a charter school, have moved the church toward more holistic forms of mission in the community. A church that was once almost entirely white and focused primarily on the needs of its members is now incredibly diverse, with no single ethnic majority present, and is trying to engage with its community in exciting new ways. In spite of the critique that I have offered regarding the current leadership and mission praxis at the church, the future is bright for The Lighthouse as it continues on its journey toward mission-actional. If Pastor Steve and the church can make the adjustments I have suggested in their leadership and mission praxis, their future could be even brighter. The missional imagination of the everyday people of God at The Lighthouse can be unleashed, and the North Port City community might experience a move of the Spirit in ways no one thought possible.

Appendix A

Interview Participants

Pastoral & Ministry Staff	Age	Gender (M/F)	Ethnicity	Marital Status (M/S)	Years on Staff	Ministry	Occupation
P1	50–55	M	Caucasian	M	20+	Pastoral Staff	Ministry
P2	50–55	F	Caucasian	M	10–15	Pastoral Staff	Ministry
P3	50–55	M	Caucasian	M	6	Pastoral Staff	Ministry
P4	40–45	F	Caucasian/ Latina	M	4	Ministry Staff	Ministry
P5	25–30	F	Caucasian	M	4	Ministry Staff	Ministry
P6	45–55	F	Pacific Islander	M	4	Ministry Staff	Ministry
P7	45–55	M	Pacific Islander	M	2	Ministry Staff	Ministry
P8	30–35	F	Panama	S	2	Ministry/ Office Staff	Staff

Appendix A: Interview Participants

Leadership Council	Age	Gender	Ethnicity	Marital Status	Years in Church	Ministry	Occupation
L1	45–55	M	African American	M	10	Children's S.S. Teacher	Management
L2	55–65	F	African American	M	16	Volunteer Deployment	Business

Lay Leaders							
L3	30–40	M	Caucasian	M	5+	Various	Missions/ Micro-enterprise
L4	45–50	F	Chinese American	M	8	Recovery Ministry	Social Worker
L5	40–45	F	Caucasian	M	11	Small Groups	CFO

Appendix B

Leadership Interview Questionnaire

1. How do you describe God's mission to the world?
2. What is the church's role in his mission? What types of things should the church be doing as it participates in God's mission?
3. How would you rate the church regarding how it is doing in this regard? Explain.
4. What has shaped your view of mission?
5. How would you describe Steve's leadership style?
6. How do you understand how decisions are actually made about whether something will happen here or not?
7. Do you need anyone's approval to try out new ideas for ministry?
8. What are the main criteria that you (or your team) use to determine as to whether God is calling you to do something?
9. How do you feel the church is doing right now including people of color in the decisions relating to its mission focus and practices?
10. What are some specific ways that the pastoral staff still needs to grow regarding multicultural issues?

Appendix C

Congregational Survey

Demographics Questions (check the appropriate box):

1. Age: ☐ under 18 ☐ 18–25 ☐ 26–35 ☐ 36–49
   ☐ 50–64 ☐ 65+

2. Sex: ☐ Male ☐ Female

3. Ethnicity/Nationality: ☐ African American ☐ Hispanic
   ☐ Asian/Pacific Islander ☐ Caucasian
   ☐ Native American ☐ African ☐ Caribbean

4. ☐ Multiracial ☐ Other _____

5. How close do you live to the church? ☐ Under 1 mile ☐ 1–3 miles
   ☐ 4–10 miles ☐ 11+ miles

6. How long have you attended The Lighthouse? ☐ Under 1 year
   ☐ 1–3 years ☐ 4–10 years ☐ 11–20 years ☐ 20+ years

7. My current level of involvement in the church (check more than one box if appropriate). ☐ Visitor
   ☐ Occasional attendee (0–2 times monthly)

8. ☐ Regular attendee (3+ times monthly) ☐ Member
   ☐ I am serving on a ministry team ☐ I am in a small group
   ☐ I am leading a ministry team

Appendix C: Congregational Survey

9. I would describe my financial status as: ☐ I/we have much more than I/we need   ☐ I/we are comfortable   ☐ I/we are barely making it   ☐ I/we often don't have enough to pay our bills   ☐ I/we receive financial assistance

10. I have lived in my current residence: ☐ Less than 1 year   ☐ 1–3 years   ☐ 4–10 years   ☐ 11+ years

11. As you take this survey, which service are you attending?
    ☐ 9:00 am   ☐ 10:30 am   ☐ 12:00 pm

Circle the letter of your response for each of the following questions. Please circle only one.

12. Which statement most accurately represents your current view about the church?
    a. I am excited about the direction our church is heading right now
    b. I feel like the church is heading in a positive direction right now
    c. I am uncertain about the direction our church is heading right now
    d. It feels like our church may be heading in the wrong the direction right now
    e. I am concerned about the direction our church is heading right now

13. What do you believe the main priority of our church should be?
    a. Providing a good Sunday morning worship experience for me and/or my family
    b. Providing compassionate ministries that will meet the needs of people in our community
    c. Helping me and/or my family to grow spiritually
    d. Providing solid programs for our youth and children
    e. Equipping me to reach my neighbors with the Gospel

Appendix C: Congregational Survey

14. If asked, most people in the community around our church would say that The Lighthouse:

    a. Is contributing significantly towards their lives and the community's well-being

    b. Is making a positive difference in their lives and the community's well-being

    c. Is having some impact on their lives and the community's well-being

    d. Is having no impact on their lives and the community's well-being

    e. I have no idea what they would say

15. Reaching people in our community with the Gospel is primarily the responsibility of our pastoral staff and other church leaders.

    a. Strongly agree

    b. Agree

    c. Neutral

    d. Disagree

    e. Strongly disagree

16. I have been approached by a leader in our church for insights into my neighbors and/or how I perceive God working in my community:

    a. Regularly

    b. Several times

    c. A few times

    d. Once

    e. Never

17. I am personally involved in the lives of my neighbors and spend meaningful time with them:

    a. Regularly (at least weekly)

    b. Often (2–3 per month)

    c. Once in a while (monthly)

Appendix C: Congregational Survey

    d. Occasionally (2–3 times per year or less)

    e. Rarely (once per year or less)

18. One of the leaders in the church has said, "Our single biggest priority is to learn how to love and serve our diverse neighbors more effectively."

    a. Strongly agree
    b. Agree
    c. Neutral
    d. Disagree
    e. Strongly disagree

19. I have an idea for reaching or serving people in our community that our church's leadership should know about.

    a. Strongly agree
    b. Agree
    c. Neutral
    d. Disagree
    e. Strongly disagree

20. I believe that the community surrounding the church should be our prime area of mission activity.

    a. Strongly agree
    b. Agree
    c. I'm not sure
    d. Disagree
    e. Strongly disagree

21. I am more involved in the lives of my neighbors and local community than I was 2–3 years ago.

    a. Definitely
    b. Somewhat
    c. About the same
    d. I am actually less involved
    e. I don't really know my neighbors that well

Appendix C: Congregational Survey

22. I believe that our church should form partnerships with individuals, local agencies and other churches to truly impact those living in our immediate community and area.

    a. Strongly agree
    b. Agree
    c. Unsure
    d. Disagree
    e. Strongly disagree

Bibliography

Alexe, C. Adelina. "The Acts of the Apostles." In *Servants and Friends: A Biblical Theology of Leadership*, edited by Skip Bell, 163–83. Berrien Springs, MI: Andrews University Press, 2014.

Barber, Benjamin R. *Consumed: How Markets Corrupt Children, Infantilize Adults, and Swallow Citizens Whole*. New York: Norton, 2007.

Barna, George. *Grow Your Church from the Outside In: Understanding the Unchurched and How to Reach Them*. Ventura, CA: Regal, 2002.

Bouma-Prediger, Steven, and Brian J. Walsh. *Beyond Homelessness: Christian Faith in a Culture of Displacement*. Grand Rapids: Eerdmans, 2008.

Branson, Mark Lau. "Ecclesiology and Leadership for the Missional Church." In *The Missional Church in Context: Helping Congregations Develop Contextual Ministry*, edited by Craig Van Gelder, 94–126. Grand Rapids: Eerdmans, 2007.

———. *Memories, Hopes, and Conversations: Appreciative Inquiry, Missional Engagement, and Congregational Change*. 2nd ed. Lanham, MD: Rowman & Littlefield, 2016.

———. "Perspectives from the Missional Conversation." In *Starting Missional Churches: Life with God in the Neighborhood*, edited by Mark Lau Branson and Nicholas Warnes, 28–47. Downers Grove, IL: InterVarsity, 2014.

Branson, Mark Lau, and Juan F. Martinez. *Churches, Cultures, and Leadership: A Practical Theology of Congregations and Ethnicities*. Downers Grove: InterVarsity Academic, 2011.

Branson, Mark Lau, and Nicholas Warnes. *Starting Missional Churches: Life with God in the Neighborhood*. Downers Grove, IL: InterVarsity, 2014.

Casey, Edward S. *The Fate of Place*. Berkeley: University of California Press, 1997.

Christerson, Brad, Korie L. Edwards, and Michael O. Emerson. *Against All Odds: The Struggle for Racial Integration in Religious Organizations*. New York: New York University Press, 2005.

Conger, Jay A., and Rabindra N. Kanungo. *Charismatic Leadership in Organizations*. Thousand Oaks, CA: Sage, 1998.

Bibliography

Cornell, Stephen, and Douglas Hartmann. *Ethnicity and Race: Making Identities in a Changing World*. 2nd ed. Sociology for a New Century. Thousand Oaks, CA: Pine Forge, 2007.

DeYoung, Curtiss Paul, et al. *United by Faith: The Multiracial Congregation as an Answer to the Problem of Race*. New York: Oxford University Press, 2003.

DiAngelo, Robin. "White Fragility." *International Journal of Critical Pedagogy* 3 (2011) 54–70.

Edwards, Korie L. *The Elusive Dream: The Power of Race in Interracial Churches*. New York: Oxford University Press, 2008.

Emerson, Michael O., and Christian Smith. *Divided by Faith: Evangelical Religion and the Problem of Race in America*. New York: Oxford University Press, 2000.

Emerson, Michael O., with Rodney M. Woo. *People of the Dream: Multiracial Congregations in the United States*. Princeton, NJ: Princeton University Press, 2006.

Feld, Steven, and Keith H. Basso, eds. *Senses of Place*. Santa Fe, NM: School of American Research, 1996.

Foster, Charles R. *Embracing Diversity: Leadership in Multicultural Congregations*. Herndon, VA: Alban Institute, 1997.

Garces-Foley, Kathleen. *Crossing the Ethnic Divide: The Multiethnic Church on a Mission*. New York: Oxford University Press, 2007.

Gornik, Mark R. *To Live in Peace: Biblical Faith and the Changing Inner City*. Grand Rapids: Eerdmans, 2002.

Gray, Derwin L. *The High Definition Leader: Building Multiethnic Churhes in a Multiethnic World*. Nashville: Thomas Nelson, 2015.

Guder, Darrell L., ed. *Missional Church: A Vision for the Sending of the Church in North America*. The Gospel and Our Culture. Grand Rapids: Eerdmanns, 1998.

Heidegger, Martin. "Building Dwelling Thinking." In *Martin Heidegger: Basic Writings*, edited by D. Krell, 319–39. New York: Harper & Row, 1977.

Heifetz, Ronald, and Marty Linsky. *Leadership on the Line: Staying Alive through the Dangers of Leading*. Boston: Harvard Business School, 2002.

Heifetz, Ronald, Alexander Grashow, and Marty Linsky. *The Practice of Adaptive Leadership: Tools and Tactics for Changing Your Organization and World*. Boston: Harvard Business School, 2009.

Hendrickson, Craig S. "Mission in an Urban Culture of Displacement: A Missional Theology of Place for the North American Church." In *God's People on the Move: Biblical and Global Perspectives on Migration and Mission*, edited by vanThanh Nguyen and John M. Prior, 101–15. Eugene, OR: Pickwick, 2014.

———. "Using Charisma to Shape Interpretive Communities in Multiethnic Congregations." *Journal of Religious Leadership* 9 (2010) 53–82.

Herrington, Jim, Mike Bonem, and James H. Furr. *Leading Congregational Change: A Practical Guide for the Transformational Journey*. San Francisco: Jossey-Bass, 2000.

Hiebert, Paul G. *Missiological Implications of Epistemological Shifts: Affirming Truth in a Modern/Postmodern World*. Christian Mission and Modern Culture. Harrisburg, PA: Trinity, 1999.

Hirsch, Alan. *The Forgotten Ways: Reactivating Apostolic Movements*. Grand Rapids: Brazos, 2006.

Humphrey, Jack. "City of Long Beach: Demographic Trends, 2001." Long Beach, CA: Eugene J. Zeller, 2001.

Inge, John. *A Christian Theology of Place*. Burlington, VT: Ashgate, 2003.

Bibliography

Johnson, Luke Timothy. *Scripture and Discernment: Decision Making in the Church*. Nashville: Abingdon, 1996.

Kahn, Miriam. "Your Place and Mine: Sharing Emotional Landscapes in Wamira, Papua New Guinea." In *Senses of Place*, edited by Steven Feld and Keith H. Basso, 167–98. Santa Fe: School of American Research, 1996.

Kujawa-Holbrook, Sheryl A. *A House of Prayer for All Nations: Congregations Building Multiracial Community*. Bethesda, MD: Alban Institute, 2002.

Law, Eric H. F. *The Wolf Shall Dwell with the Lamb: A Spirituality for Leadership in a Multicultural Community*. St. Louis: Chalice, 1993.

Leong, David P. *Race and Place: How Urban Geography Shapes the Journey to Reconciliation*. Downers Grove, IL: InterVarsity, 2017.

Livermore, David A. *Cultural Intelligence: Improving Your CQ to Engage Our Multicultural World*. Youth, Family, and Culture. Grand Rapids: Baker Academic, 2009.

Loritts, Bryan. *Right Color, Wrong Culture: The Type of Leader Your Organization Needs to Become Multiethnic: A Leadership Fable*. Chicago: Moody, 2014.

Low, Setha M., and Denise Lawrence-Zuniga, eds. *The Anthropology of Space and Place: Locating Culture*. Malden, MA: Blackwell, 2003.

Malphurs, Aubrey. *Developing a Vision for Ministry in the Twenty-First Century*. Grand Rapids: Baker, 1999.

Marston, Leslie Ray. *From Age to Age a Living Witness: Free Methodism's First Century*. Indianapolis: Wesleyan, 1997.

McGavran, Donald, and C. Peter Wagner. *Understanding Church Growth*. 3rd ed. Grand Rapids: Eerdmans, 1990.

Metzger, Paul L. *Consuming Jesus: Beyond Race and Class Divisions in a Consumer Church*. Grand Rapids: Eerdmans, 2007.

Moltmann, Jurgen. *The Church in the Power of the Spirit: A Contribution to Messianic Ecclesiology*. London: SCM, 1977.

Ortiz, Manuel. *One New People: Models for Developing a Multiethnic Church*. Downers Grove, IL: InterVarsity, 1996.

Rainer, Thom S. *The Book of Church Growth: History, Theology, and Principles*. Nashville: Broadman & Holman, 1993.

Rainer, Thom S., and Eric Gieger. *Simple Church: Returning to God's Process for Making Disciples*. Updated ed. Nashville: Broadman & Holman, 2011.

Rodman, Margaret. "Empowering Place: Multilocality and Multivocality." In *The Anthropology of Space and Place: Locating Culture*, edited by Setha M. Low and Denise Lawrence-Zuniga, 204–23. Malden, MA: Blackwell, 2003.

Roxburgh, Alan. *Missional: Joining God in the Neighborhood*. Grand Rapids: Baker, 2011.

———. *Missional Map-Making: Skills for Leading in Times of Transition*. Jossey-Bass Leadership. San Francisco: Jossey-Bass, 2010.

Roxburgh, Alan, and Fred Romanuk. *The Missional Leader: Equipping Your Church To Reach a Changing World*. San Francisco: Jossey-Bass, 2006.

Rusaw, Rick, and Eric Swanson. *The Externally Focused Church*. Loveland, CO: Group, 2004.

Sanders, Alvin. *Bridging the Diversity Gap: Leading Toward God's Multiethnic Kingdom*. Indianapolis: Wesleyan, 2013.

Smith, Efrem. *The Post-Black and Post-White Church: Becoming the Beloved Community in a Multiethnic World*. Leadership Network. San Francisco: Jossey-Bass, 2012.

Bibliography

Soja, Edward W. *Postmodern Geographies: The Reassertion of Space in Critical Social Theory.* New York: Verso, 1989.
Southerland, Dan. *Transitioning: Leading Your Church Through Change.* Littleton, CO: Serendipity, 1999.
Strauss, Claudia, and Naomi Quinn. *A Cognitive Theory of Cultural Meaning.* Cambridge: Cambridge University Press, 1998.
Tatum, Beverly Daniel. *Why Are All the Black Kids Sitting Together in the Cafeteria? And Other Conversations about Race.* New York: Basic, 1997.
US Census Bureau. "American Community Survey." 2015. https://data.census.gov/cedsci/table?q=Long%20Beach,%20CA&lastDisplayedRow=80&table=DP05&tid=ACSDP1Y2015.DP05&g=1600000US0643000.
Van Gelder, Craig. *The Ministry of the Missional Church: A Community Led by the Spirit.* Grand Rapids: Baker, 2007.
———, ed. *The Missional Church in Context: Helping Congregations Develop Contextual Ministry.* Grand Rapids: Baker, 2007.
Van Gelder, Craig, and Dwight J. Zscheile. *The Missional Church in Perspective: Mapping Trends and Shaping the Conversation.* Grand Rapids: Baker Academic, 2011.
Wagner, C. Peter. *Church Growth and the Whole Gospel: A Biblical Mandate.* San Francisco: Harper & Row, 1981.
Warnes, Nicholas. "Shifting Perceptions on How We Plant Churches." In *Starting Missional Churches: Life with God in the Neighborhood*, edited by Mark Lau Branson and Nicholas Warnes, 13–27. Downers Grove, IL: InterVarsity, 2014.
Warren, Rick. *The Purpose Driven Church: Growth without Compromising your Message and Mission.* Grand Rapids: Zondervan, 1995.
Yancey, George. *One Body One Spirit: Principles of Successful Multiracial Churches.* Downers Grove, IL: InterVarsity, 2003.
Yin, Robert K. *Case Study Research: Design and Methods.* Edited by Leonard Bickman and Debra J. Rog. 4th ed. Applied Social Research Methods. Thousand Oaks, CA: Sage, 2009.
Zscheile, Dwight J. *The Agile Church: Spirit-Led Innovation in an Uncertain Age.* New York: Morehouse, 2014.
———. "The Trinity, Leadership, and Power." *Journal of Religious Leadership* 6 (2007) 43–63.

www.ingramcontent.com/pod-product-compliance
Lightning Source LLC
Chambersburg PA
CBHW051942160426
43198CB00013B/2262